HOLLYWOOD MONEY TRAPS

What Every Investor Needs To Know

By

Alexia Melocchi

International Film Producer

Author of "An Insiders Secret: Mastering the Hollywood Path"
&
"The Heart of Show Business: Your Road Map to Hollywood"

Published by Little Studio Films

ISBN: 979-8-9957353-3-5
LCCN: 2026912396

Edited by: Heidi Stangeland
Cover by: Mark Moorer

DEDICATION

To my mother and business partner Alexandra — who always told it like it is. To my three cats — who show me unconditional love every single day. And to Debbie — who showed me how to harness the power of words for my journey here on Earth.

Advanced Praise

"Hollywood Money Traps: What Every Film Investor Needs to Know" is an essential, must-read book, written by Alexia Melocchi, that every film producer needs to read. It helps Producers and Directors navigate the complicated world of production financing and distribution."

Marty Katz, *Producer and former Executive Vice President 20th Century Fox and Walt Disney*

"Alexia takes your hand and transforms into your mentor from the very first pages. She has created a valuable guide for producers, investors and creatives where she offers a wealth of insider tips, through her personal life stories, ultimately encouraging her audience to master the art of asking better questions."

Sofia Eleftheriades, *Entertainment industry specialist in global film sales and strategy*

"Some investors think the "business" end of "show business" is a labyrinth where their money will inevitably be lost. Alexia's cautionary tales-told from the front lines of the negotiations-shine a light on the money trail, offering a clear and reliable path forward.   Invest in this book first!"

Joseph Busch, *former Vice President, Distribution, MGM and Sony Pictures Television*

"Alexia's book is a must-read for any film investor. With her vast knowledge in film distribution and production, she gives you the tools to truly educate yourself and assess your risks before putting your money into a project and avoid the misconception of film investment. "

Karinne Behr, *Finance in Motion*

"Alexia is a rare force in the film industry — someone who seamlessly embodies the roles of producer, creator, international sales agent, and manager of talented filmmakers. Fluent in multiple languages and deeply attuned to the complexities of working across different countries, she brings a truly global perspective. This book is a must-read, as she generously shares decades of invaluable experience and insight. "

Michel Vandewalle, *Atlas International Germany*

TABLE OF CONTENTS

Why Hollywood Investing Is So Misunderstood

I am an investor, just like you.

I know what it feels like to believe in something so much that you put everything on the line for it. I came to this country from Italy as a teenager with $5,000, two suitcases, with my single mother. I had no roadmap, no connections, and no safety net — only a fierce determination to build something real in America. Because of the languages I spoke, I found my way into the international distribution business of film and television almost by accident, hired as a translator for an international movie buyer. There were no mentors, no formal training — just the school of hard knocks and a relentless drive to figure it out. I started my own international sales company at the age of 19, selling independent films across the world at the major film markets and festivals, alongside my mother, who became my business partner.

My job was simple and non-negotiable: every movie I was entrusted to sell had to make its money back, plus profit.

That discipline helped me make my first million dollars by the age of twenty.

Over the decades that followed, I wore every hat this industry has to offer. I have been a producer, a creator, an international sales agent, a manager of talented filmmakers, and a representative of major international distributors. I have sat across the table from buyers pre-purchasing films at the script stage — bankable contracts that functioned, in every real sense, as investments — and I guided them through the process of protecting those acquisitions. I have advised and consulted both investors and filmmakers. And I have been burned myself. I am not writing this book from a safe distance. I have made my own share of mistakes — working with the wrong partners, the wrong sales companies, the wrong assumptions.

My greatest professional obligation, the one that kept me up at night, was ensuring that anyone who believed in me and trusted me with their money would get it back.

Many of them did. Not all of them.

That is why this book exists.

Throughout my career, I watched a pattern repeat itself with heartbreaking consistency.

Passionate filmmakers — many of them talented, most of them well-intentioned — would approach investors and paint a picture of red carpets, celebrity encounters, multi-million-dollar deals, and life-changing returns. Sometimes the exaggeration was deliberate. More often, it came from a place of pure passion and genuine ignorance about how the business actually works. Either way, the investor paid the price.

To this day, filmmakers come to me regularly, asking me to sell their finished films or to lend my reputation to their projects so they can attract more funding. And it is quite common that when I look at what they've built — the contracts, the agreements, the promises made to the people who backed them — I cringe.

The mistakes are glaring. The misrepresentations are real. The investors who said yes had no idea what they were

agreeing to, and so I politely decline. I cannot put my name on that.

Somewhere out there, an investor is still waiting to see a return that will never come.

This happens because there is no shortage of books telling filmmakers how to find investors, how to pitch them, how to get them to write a check. But nobody has written the book for the person holding the pen.

Until now.

And who are these investors? They are not Wall Street professionals with legal teams and financial analysts. They are friends and family. People using credit cards, savings accounts, even their IRAs. People who wanted to see their name on a big screen. People who wanted to attend a premiere and feel part of something extraordinary. People who loved the art of storytelling and wanted to support it — and who trusted, perhaps too easily, the person asking them to write a check.

This book is for them.

For more than two decades, I have shared the insider realities of this industry through my podcast, The Heart of Show Business, which has become a trusted resource for film and television professionals worldwide. My previous books — An Insider's Secret: Mastering the Hollywood Path and The Heart of Show Business: Your Road Map to Hollywood — were written for the creatives: the filmmakers, the actors, the storytellers trying to navigate one of the most complex industries on earth.

This book crosses the line. This one is for the people who back those creatives. The investors. The believers. The ones whose money makes the movies possible — and who deserve to be protected.

Today, storytelling is one of the most valuable commodities in the world.

The demand for content has never been higher. There has never been a better or more legitimate reason to consider film and television as part of an investment strategy. But wanting to support the arts does not mean surrendering your judgment — or your savings. The sophisticated

investment firms already have teams to protect them: lawyers, business managers, fact-checkers who know exactly what questions to ask. When you don't have that infrastructure around you, you need something else.

You need this book.

What follows is not a collection of theories or academic frameworks. It is a guide built from thirty years of lived experience — deals gone wrong, contracts misread, promises broken, and hard lessons learned across every seat at the table. It is told through real stories, with the specific traps named and explained so that you can recognize them before they find you.

So many books exist to help filmmakers get your money. This is the first one written to help you protect it- while still being part of the magic.

Let's begin.

Chapter 1 –
The Deal That Nearly Ruined Us

Chain-of-Title and Ownership Chaos

Every lesson I have ever learned about film investment —
the hard ones, the ones that stick — can be traced back to a
single phone call that shook my world.

But let me start at the beginning.

By 1990, my mother and I had built something we were
genuinely proud of.

Axelia International Pictures was our company — a
mother-daughter, all-women-owned international sales
operation at a time when that combination was virtually
unheard of in the film industry. We had spent several
successful years selling finished films, every single one of
them to profit. Our secret was simple: we understood
people. We spoke multiple languages, we respected the
cultures of the buyers we worked with, and we believed
deeply in the power of storytelling. In a business full of
smoke and bluster, that authenticity opened doors.

We were thriving. And then a project arrived that changed
everything.

It came to us through a producer we respected — a man who had worked for Michael Douglas's company, with real credentials and real relationships.

He brought us a passion project: a World War II story set in Poland, based on true events, with a major casting director already attached and a roster of A-list actors that included Christopher Reeve. It was the kind of material that makes you catch your breath. A true story. Serious subject matter. Serious talent. It was called *Midnight Spy.*

There was one complication: there was no financing in place yet. But the producer had assurances from the Polish director that a portion of the funding was already secured in Poland. The plan was to take the film to market, generate pre-sales from international distributors, and use those bankable contracts to bridge the gap and get the film into production. It was a legitimate model. We had done it before.

We believed in this one completely.

So we committed. We invested significant company funds into the project— including what I believe was one of the earliest examples of what the industry now calls a Teaser Trailer or mood reel. Today you can cut something like that on a laptop for next to nothing. In 1990, we paid 15,000 to produce it on film, with raw footage and music, and a top Hollywood narrator, designed to convey the tone and soul of the story. It was ahead of its time, and we were proud of it.

We took everything to Cannes. We bought space for a large poster outside the Martinez Hotel. The film became the buzz of the market — the cast, the story, the material all spoke for themselves. Within that first debut at the festival, we had generated serious interest from multiple major international distribution companies. Pre-sale offers were on the table.

We left Cannes with the ammunition he needed to go back to his investor network and close the rest of the financing. We thought we had hit the jackpot.

Then the phone rang.

Back home, while the major trade publications like Variety and The Hollywood Reporter announced the film, a series of individuals began reaching out to us. Strangers. Each one with a version of the same story: they had given money to the director. Some said they had lent it to him personally. Others said he had promised them ownership stakes in the film. The amounts they described were not small — we were talking about hundreds of thousands of dollars, spread across multiple people, none of whom had any formal documentation that would hold up to scrutiny.

As we pieced the picture together, the truth became impossible to ignore. The director had been quietly raising money for years — giving out shares of a film company that barely existed, making promises about returns the moment the movie went into production. And the money raised had not gone into the film. It had gone into his life. His bills. His lifestyle.

When we did the math, the project was dead. The debt load behind it was so significant that no legitimate production could absorb it. Every pre-sale we had worked so hard to secure at Cannes was now useless.

Every relationship we had leveraged — with distributors, with the cast, with our buyers — was now awkward and exposed. We had to go back to those distributors and quietly redirect them toward other projects. We walked away from something we had invested in financially, professionally, and emotionally.

It was the most expensive education of my career. And I never forgot a single lesson.

I will tell you how disturbed we were by that phone call: my mother, my business partner, my anchor in this industry — she got physically sick and threw up.

In the aftermath, half-joking and completely serious at the same time, she announced that she was going to write a book called *No More Movies — I Would Rather Have a Life.* The book never got written. But this story was always going to be part of it.

My mother went on to channel all that passion, resilience, and hard-won wisdom into something else entirely. Today she is a bestselling author — her book "Machiavelli Princess " stands as proof that the best stories find their way out eventually, one way or another. As for the movie industry? We never left. Some loves are just too complicated to walk away from.

What This Story Teaches Every Investor

1. **The film existed on paper. The company did not.**

The director had been selling shares of a production entity that had no legal foundation, no audited accounts, and no chain-of-title documentation. Investors were handed promises, not contracts. Before you invest a single dollar in any film or television project, you must verify that the production company is a legally registered entity, that it owns or controls the rights to the material, and that any shares being offered are backed by a real operating agreement — reviewed by an entertainment attorney.

2. Buzz and Hype are not the same as a greenlight.

The fact that distributors expressed interest at Cannes meant the project had potential. It did not mean the film was being made. It did not mean investor money was protected. Enthusiasm at a film market is a signal, not a guarantee.

Many investors confuse the excitement of a marketplace moment — a poster, a trade announcement, a famous name attached — with confirmation that production is imminent and their money is safe. It is not.

3. Hidden debt kills films before cameras ever roll.

The single most dangerous thing we discovered was not that the director had made promises — it was that those promises were invisible to us until it was too late. Every film project carries a financial history. Before investing, you must ask for a complete accounting of all prior commitments, loans, deferred payments, and ownership agreements related to the project. If that documentation is incomplete, unavailable, or met with resistance, walk away.

4. Shares in an unmade film may be worth nothing.

Investors in this project were told they owned a piece of something.

What they owned was a percentage of a heavily indebted, legally tangled entity with no clear path to production.

Even if the film had eventually been made, those early investors would have found themselves at the back of a very long line — behind the bank, behind the completion bond, behind the sales agent, behind deferred fees. Your percentage of a film is only as valuable as what comes before you in the waterfall. Always ask: who gets paid first, and where exactly do I stand in line?

5. The glamour of the project is the trap.

Christopher Reeve. A true World War II story. The Martinez Hotel. The buzz of Cannes. Every one of those details was real — and every one of them was used, consciously or not, to create an emotional environment in which asking hard financial questions felt almost rude. The more exciting a project feels, the more disciplined you must be about separating the story you are told from the story in the spreadsheet.

There is a rule I apply to every project I am involved with today.

Whether I am lending my name, selling a film, or producing, I require that investors have the opportunity to meet the key team members and ask their questions directly. Not just the producer who is pitching them. Not just the person they trust. Everyone — the director, the sales agent, the key creatives.

As an investor, you should demand the same. If someone is asking you to write a check, you have every right to sit in a room — virtual or otherwise — with every significant person attached to that project and ask them anything you want. How they respond to that request will tell you almost everything you need to know. Confidence, transparency, and preparation are the marks of a team worth backing. Hesitation, deflection, or excuses are the marks of a team that has something to hide.

You are not being difficult. You are being a responsible investor.

Chapter 2 –
The Dog and Pony Show Where There Was No Dog nor Pony

When Smoke and Mirrors Replace a Finished Film

There is a moment in this business when the illusion cracks — when everything you were sold turns out to be a carefully constructed performance with nothing behind it. I experienced that moment early in my career, on one of the first movies we sold, and I have never forgotten the particular mix of horror, fury, and clarity it produced.

It was 1989, and Axelia International Pictures was still finding its footing in the marketplace. One of the very first films we agreed to represent came to us through an entertainment attorney we trusted and respected. He arrived with a partner — a music producer with an impressive roster, a man who had represented some of the greatest artists of the 50s.

Together they brought us an action film.
Shot in the desert.
Full of explosions, beautiful women in commando uniforms, guns, and the kind of kinetic energy that

practically leaped off the screen.

In those days — and I say this with full awareness of how it sounds — the formula for international sales was not complicated. If you had attractive women, gunfire, and car explosions, distributors would walk into your office with figurative suitcases full of money. The poster alone for this film had everything: striking imagery, undeniable visual impact. The trailer delivered explosions and spectacle in equal measure. It was the kind of package that sells itself.

They told us the film was in production and nearly complete. The director and his gorgeous cast — all of them striking — were going to fly into the festival and make their presence felt. They would walk the Croisette Boardwalk generate buzz, send buyers to our offices. It was going to be a show. The attention it drew was immediate and intense.

Our biggest sale was to Japan. All deals concluded were close to a million dollars — significant money at any point in this industry, extraordinary for a company as young as ours. More remarkably, the Japanese distributor handed us a big deposit on the spot, right there.

That almost never happens. We were elated. We had done our jobs.

Then we asked to see the finished picture.

The stalling began immediately. Message after message from the attorney, each one offering a new reason why the film was not quite ready. They were still working on it. Just a little more time. We were patient. We had a relationship with these people. We trusted the process. Finally, we were invited to a screening. We were so excited that we had nearly arranged for our Japanese distributor to join us — to celebrate the deal.

Thank God he was not available that day.

I want you to understand what it felt like to sit in that screening room. We walked in proud. We had made a significant sale. We had represented something that felt real and commercial and exciting. We were ready to watch our work pay off.

What we saw instead will stay with me for the rest of my life.

The first ten or fifteen minutes of the film were exactly what we had sold — the footage from the trailer, polished and professional and full of production value.

And then it changed.

The rest of the film — the vast majority of it — had been shot on video. Not film. Video. With unknown actors reading their lines off pieces of paper held just outside the frame. No production design. No lighting. No craft of any kind. It looked like something a ten-year-old had filmed in an afternoon.

We had sold a trailer. The film did not exist.
We were horrified. And then we were furious. And then, very quickly, we got to work.

At the screening, we handed the entertainment attorney had a check at the screening — as some gesture of good faith or celebration. The moment we understood what we had just watched, we took it back.
Physically. We told him clearly: we are returning this money to our distributors. You are not keeping it.

We called every distributor who had purchased the film. We asked for their banking information. And we returned every deposit, in full, without hesitation, without attempting to negotiate or redirect the funds elsewhere.

In an industry where that money would routinely have been kept, argued over, or quietly absorbed into other costs, we gave it back.

What happened next surprised even us.

The Japanese distributor — the one who had given us the largest deposit, in a culture where business relationships are formal, where women are rarely treated as equals, where a handshake is replaced by a bow — became one of our most loyal and devoted partners.

From that moment forward, whenever we crossed paths at a film market anywhere in the world, the CEO of that company would find us in the crowd. And he would give us hugs. Kisses on the cheek. The kind of warmth that transcends business entirely.

Integrity travels further than any sale ever could.

We lost the commission on nearly a million dollars in deals that day. We gained something worth far more — a reputation that preceded us into every room we walked into for the next thirty years.

What This Story Teaches Every Investor

1. **Never invest all of your money upfront in a film in production that you have not yet seen finished.**

The single most important structural protection you have as an investor is staged disbursement. Do not release the full investment in one lump sum at the beginning. Instead, tie every payment to a verified milestone — script delivery, first day of principal photography, picture lock, sound mix, final delivery.

Have an independent accountant or escrow agent manage the disbursements, releasing funds only when each stage has been confirmed and documented. In this story, the fraud would have been discovered long before a million dollars was at stake had the money been tied to delivery of a verifiable, completed film.

2. **Invest in stages. See progress before releasing the next payment.**

Staged investment is not a sign of distrust — it is standard practice in every serious creative industry. A legitimate production team will welcome it because it holds everyone accountable and creates a clean paper trail. If a producer resists staged payments and insists on receiving the full budget upfront, that resistance is itself a warning sign. Ask yourself: what are they afraid you will notice as long as you invest it all?

3. The show around a film is not the film.

Beautiful people at a marketplace. A striking poster. An impressive trailer. All of these are marketing — and marketing can be constructed around almost anything, including a project that is fundamentally incomplete. The spectacle designed to attract buyers and investors is specifically engineered to bypass your skepticism. The more dazzling the presentation, the more carefully you should look at what lies behind it.

4. Stalling is a red flag, not a scheduling issue.

When the people you are working with consistently delay showing you the product — the finished film, the completed cut, the verified footage, the signed agreements — that pattern is telling you something is not ready, not right, or not real. Legitimate productions with nothing to hide do not stall. They invite scrutiny. If you are being kept from seeing what your money is attached to, start asking hard questions.

5. For smaller investments, ask to share ownership of the copyright as collateral.

If your investment is under one million dollars, a formal completion bond may not be practical or available. Instead, negotiate to have the film's copyright assigned to you as collateral for the duration of your investment. This gives you a legally recognized security interest in the underlying intellectual property — meaning that if the production fails to deliver, you have something tangible to show for your money. Make sure this is documented in writing by an entertainment attorney, not simply promised verbally.

6. **For investments over one million dollars, require a completion bond and a contingency budget**.

At this level of investment, a completion bond — an insurance instrument that guarantees the film will be delivered on time and to specification — becomes a realistic and necessary requirement.

Equally important is a properly structured contingency line in the budget, typically ten to fifteen percent of the total, set aside specifically to cover unexpected costs. A budget with no contingency is a budget built on optimism rather than experience. Both the bond and the contingency protect you from the most common production failure: a film that runs out of money before it runs out of story.

7. **Integrity is the only currency that never loses its value.**

In this story, we lost a commission representing nearly a million dollars in sales. We returned it anyway — immediately, completely, and without negotiation — because our relationships and our reputation mattered more than the money. That decision compounded over decades into something no single deal could ever have produced. As an investor, look for partners who operate this way. They are rarer than you think, and worth every premium.

Chapter 3 –
The Rights That Were Never Ours

Option Fraud and the Producer Who Played Both Sides

And then you are betrayed but someone you inherently trust, because of their main profession who destroy the path of a project because they should have known better.

This story takes us back to the early 1990s, to what I still think of as the golden age of international film sales. The marketplace was alive with possibility. Relationships were built on handshakes and reputation. And Axelia International Pictures was at the height of its momentum, representing some of the most exciting independent projects in the world.

A producer came to us with a project that was genuinely exceptional.

Based on a celebrated literary piece, it had everything we looked for: a compelling story, a recently Oscar-nominated actor at the peak of his profile, a rising actress generating real industry attention, and a talented British director whose vision for the material was clear and confident.

The producers were a husband-and-wife team. He was an entertainment attorney.

I want to pause on that detail — that he was an attorney — because it matters to what comes later. When a lawyer brings you a project, there is an implicit assurance that accompanies it. You assume the legal architecture is sound. You assume the rights have been properly secured. You assume that someone who drafts contracts for a living would never hand you a project built on a foundation that could collapse at any moment. That assumption, it turned out, was exactly the trap.

We took the project to Milan, Italy for MIFED (one of the biggest European trade shows for film). We invested significantly in our promotional presence with materials designed to make the project impossible to ignore. The strategy worked. Within that market we connected with a prominent British producer, a man with deep industry relationships who immediately understood the potential of the material.

He loved the director. He loved the cast. He wanted in and was bringing on board a major British broadcaster.

We were positioned not just as international sales agents but FINALLY as executive producers — the people who had assembled the pieces, invested our own resources, and were actively pre-selling the film to build the financing bridge that would get it made.

We came home from a Film Market that always brought us great luck and business deals, with the kind of momentum that makes you believe everything is possible. The UK partnership was taking shape. Pre-sales were generating real deposits. The film felt inevitable. Instead of thanking us for our work, the producer- the attorney called to tell us there was a problem. The agent representing the writer of the original literary piece had been in touch. The option agreement — the legal contract giving the producers the right to adapt the work into a film — was expiring.

And the agent, fully aware that financing had been raised and production was imminent, had decided this was the ideal moment to apply pressure. Twenty thousand dollars, or the option would lapse and the rights would be lost. We were stunned. Not by the agent's maneuver — that kind of leverage play, however uncomfortable, exists in the industry — but by the fact that we were hearing about it at all.

An attorney producer who had been developing this project for long enough to bring us in so we could generate pre-sales, attract UK partners, and build real momentum had apparently allowed the option to run down to its final days without renewal. How was that possible?

We asked him to renew it immediately. The UK partners were ready. The money was moving. Twenty thousand dollars to protect everything we had built together was not a difficult decision.

One problem: He did not have the money.

I remember sitting with my mother after that call, trying to make sense of it. Here was an attorney. A man who had chosen to become a film producer, with a project, watched us invest our time and money and reputation into making it real, stood beside us at Cannes as we built something genuinely exciting — and now was telling us he needed us to write a personal check to save the rights he was supposed to have already secured.

The emotional logic of it was suffocating. We had skin in the game. We had relationships on the line. We had pre-sales sitting on deposits that depended on this film existing. Walking away was not a clean option. And he knew that. Whether it was calculated or simply desperate, the effect was the same: we were being squeezed.

We wrote the check. Twenty thousand dollars, drawn from the advances and deposits we had earned through our pre-sales.

Money that represented our work, our investment, our executive producer stake in the project. We gave it to him with the explicit understanding that it would go directly to the writer's agent to renew the option. He confirmed it was done. He told us the option had been signed. We exhaled and moved forward.

Then the writer's agent called us directly.
He had received nothing. The option had not been renewed. The rights were still lapsing.

When we confronted the producer, he offered an explanation I no longer even remember — because whatever it was, it did not matter. The money was gone. The rights were gone. The UK partnership, the pre-sales, the momentum, the poster on the wall at Cannes — all of it dissolved. We had been lied to by a man whose professional identity was built on the law. And we had no recourse that would not cost us more than we had already lost.

We lost the money. We lost the project. And we carried the embarrassment of having to explain to our UK partners and our pre-sale buyers why a film we had championed so confidently had simply ceased to exist.

What we did not lose was the lesson. And it is one we have never had to learn twice.

What This Story Teaches Every Investor

1. **Always verify that the rights are secured — and for long enough**.

A film cannot be legally produced, sold, or distributed without the producer owning or controlling the rights to

the underlying material.

Before any money moves — yours or anyone else's — ask to see the option agreement or rights purchase contract. Confirm it is current, signed by all parties, and has sufficient time remaining to allow for a realistic production timeline. In this industry, putting a film together takes years, not months. An option that expires in six months is not protection — it is a ticking clock.

Require a minimum of two years on any option attached to a project you are investing in, with clear renewal provisions in place.

2. Get copies of every rights agreement yourself.

Do not rely on being told the rights are secured. Do not rely on a producer's assurances, however credible they seem. Do not rely on the fact that the producer is also an attorney. Ask for a copy of the actual option or rights agreement, have your own entertainment lawyer review it, and confirm directly with the rights holder or their representative that the agreement is active and in good standing.

3. A professional title does not guarantee professional conduct.

An attorney who becomes a producer does not automatically bring the rigor of the law to the chaos of film production. A studio executive who starts an independent company does not automatically produce at a studio level. A doctor who writes a thriller does not automatically know how to protect his investment. In every chapter of this book, the most expensive mistakes have been made by people who carried impressive credentials into situations those credentials did not actually cover.

Judge every person by their specific, verifiable track record in the role they are currently occupying — not by the titles they have held elsewhere.

4. Emotional blackmail is a business tool — recognize it and resist it.

The pressure we felt in this story was real. We had relationships at stake. We had partners in the UK who were counting on us. We had pre-sales that depended on the film existing. Walking away from the twenty-thousand-dollar demand would have meant walking away from everything we had built. That is not an accident — that is the mechanism of emotional blackmail. The more you have invested in a project, the more leverage someone has over you when they create a crisis. Recognize this dynamic the moment it appears.

When someone puts you in a position where you feel you have no choice but to give them money to protect what you have already spent, slow down.

5. Ask questions. Verify before you pay.

Writers, agents, and the full rights chain must be part of the conversation from day one.

One of the lessons we took from this experience was the importance of establishing direct communication with every party in the rights chain — not just the producer.

The writer's agent in this story was not the villain. They were simply protecting their client in a situation where the option was genuinely expiring. Had we known the timeline, we could have acted. Had the producer been transparent with the writer and agent about the length of the process and what it realistically required, a negotiated extension might have been possible without the crisis.

Everyone in the chain — writer, agent, producer, sales agent, financier — needs to understand the timeline and agree to it.

6. Surprises at the eleventh hour are almost always avoidable.

Never advance personal funds to cover a producer's failed obligations.

This is a boundary that must be established clearly and held firmly.

Your role as an investor is to finance the film — not to rescue the producer from their own failures of planning or disclosure.

The moment you are asked to cover costs that the producer was responsible for securing independently — whether that is an option renewal, a crew deposit, a location fee, or any other obligation — you have moved from investor to guarantor. That is a fundamentally different risk profile, and it rarely ends well. If a producer cannot meet their own basic obligations, ask yourself what else they have not told you.

Chapter 4 –
When One Film Became Two

Creative Bait-and-Switch

It was the early 2000s, and for the first time in my career, I was stepping into a role I had never played before: full producer.

I had spent years as a highly respected international sales agent, executive producer, and buyers' representative. I knew how to sell films. I knew how to read a market. I knew how to get a movie in front of the right distributors anywhere in the world. But producing — the day-to-day financial and creative oversight of actually making a film — that was new territory for me. This new territory was a must to enter into, as in earlier years our sales agent role had naturally evolved into all the things a producer does- from casting advice to script notes, to marketing strategies. We now wanted the recognition of our creative input from script to screen.

It started with a book. A doctor — a man with no film industry background but a vivid imagination — submitted his medical thriller manuscript to us. The material was genuinely compelling, and I saw the potential immediately. I suggested he convert it into a screenplay and connected him with a director I represented, someone with a strong visual voice and the right sensibility for the story.

The pieces came together quickly. The doctor caught the filmmaking bug. He wanted to watch his story come to life on screen, and he had the means to make it happen.

He told me he had five or six close friends — fellow doctors — who were willing to back the project together. Not professional investors. People who believed in their friend, loved the story, and wanted to be part of something creative and memorable. The financing was real, the director was ready, the script was solid. All we needed was an experienced producer who had done it before, to bring it home.

Because I was new to producing, I reached out to someone I knew from the industry — a person who had worked at a well-known production company based inside a major studio. His title there had been Head of Development, which sounded authoritative.

But the reality was more modest: his primary function had been reading scripts and passing recommendations up the chain as a low-level creative executive. He had recently left to become a partner in a new, independent production company — and it was in that new capacity that I brought him in.

I liked him. I liked his partner. And when I presented them with the project — a finished screenplay, an attached director, a motivated investor with funds ready to go — they were confident and persuasive. They assured me they could deliver the film within the intended budget.
They spoke of relationships, of favors owed, of their ability to attract strong actors and good crew at favorable rates. It all sounded credible.

It all sounded like exactly what we needed.
So I made the introduction. The investor met them, was impressed, and the money began to move. We had assembled what looked like a complete team: the doctor's story, my director, their production infrastructure, and a budget everyone had agreed upon. What could go wrong?

Quite a lot, as it turned out.

The first thing I noticed — too late — was the casting. The producers had promised relationships that would bring in actors with real commercial appeal, names that would help sell the film internationally.

What we got instead were actors chosen largely on the basis of personal favors — people they owed something to, or who owed something to them.

Not the names I would have selected. Not the names that would open doors with distributors. The casting served the producers' internal relationships, not the film's commercial future.

I raised my concerns. But by then, the money was already in. Pre-production was underway. The crew was hired, the schedule was set, and the momentum of a film about to shoot is a force that is almost impossible to reverse. We had made the introductions, connected all the pieces, and then — gradually, almost imperceptibly — been moved to the back seat. And once you are in the back seat with the money already flowing, you cannot easily stop the car.

As the investor funds came in and production bills began arriving, we did not scrutinize every line with the rigor we should have. We trusted. We assumed that costs being submitted were legitimate expenses for our film. What we discovered afterward told a different story.

The funds entrusted to us for this one production had been

quietly spread across not one, not two, but three projects. Our investor's money — given in good faith to bring a single medical thriller to life — had helped finance two additional small films the production company was developing on the side. No disclosure. No permission. No conversation.

It was a betrayal dressed up as business as usual.

The film itself turned out well. The director delivered. The story was told. But the budget had been carved up, which left nothing for marketing — and a film with no marketing budget is a film that disappears. Then came distribution: I recommended that we handle it ourselves, leveraging our years of relationships and market expertise.

Instead, the investor deferred to the producers, who steered the film toward a company that made impressive promises and delivered almost none of them. The film was undersold. The investors saw almost nothing back.

They lost twice. Once in production. Once in distribution. And at every turn, the decisions that hurt them most were made by people who performed confidence rather than earned it.

I still feel the weight of that. He never fully recouped his investment.

I believe that for him, seeing his story made into a film mattered more than the money — and perhaps that is the grace that softened the blow.

But he deserved both. He deserved the experience and the return. Every investor does.

I still think about the day the doctor flew in to visit the set with his friends. I made sure it was everything he had dreamed of —introductions to the cast, time with the actors, a real behind-the-scenes experience that money alone cannot buy. He was glowing. His friends were glowing. For them, in that moment, the investment had already paid off in a way that had nothing to do with returns. They were inside the world of their story. That memory stays with me.

But something else happened on that visit that I have never forgotten. When he sat down with the producers and the investors for a celebration dinner, I watched the dynamic shift in a way that made my stomach drop. Any opinion expressed by us or question from the investor was answered in vague manner. They spoke in half-sentences and let long silences do the work for them. And instead of turning to me — the person who had found the project, built the team, and understood the business — he leaned toward them. He was impressed by their silence. He mistook it for power.

That was the moment I knew I had lost control. Not because I lacked the expertise.
But because appearances of perceived power had overridden quiet, earned authority. I knew the business. They knew how to perform it.
And in that room, performance won.

What This Story Teaches Every Investor

1. Verify every dollar — every single one.

When you invest in a film, you are entitled to a full, itemized budget and the right to approve or audit how those funds are spent. Do not assume. Do not trust without verifying.

Require regular financial reporting and insist that every significant expenditure be documented and justified. Your money was given for one specific purpose. Make sure it is being used for exactly that.

2. One investment means one film.

Unless you have explicitly agreed in writing to finance multiple projects, your money belongs to one production only. Any redirection of investor funds — however small, however well-intentioned — to another project without full disclosure and written consent is a misuse of capital. Ensure your investment agreement specifies this clearly, and that any deviation requires your explicit written approval.

3. A title is not the same as experience.

Head of Development, Executive Producer, Studio Associate — these titles can represent decades of genuine mastery, or they can be largely ceremonial. The man in this story had read scripts and passed recommendations up the chain. That is a valuable skill, but it is not the same as having produced a film from budget to delivery.
Before you trust anyone with your money, ask for a specific, verifiable track record. What films have they actually produced from start to finish? What were the budgets? What were the results?

Then verify those answers independently.

4. **Casting affects your return** — ask who is being cast and why.

The actors attached to a film are not just creative decisions — they are commercial ones. Certain names open doors with distributors. Others do not.

When casting is driven by internal favors and personal relationships rather than market strategy, it is the investor who pays the price in reduced sales potential. Before production begins, ask: who are the lead actors, what is their international market value, and who made the casting decision and on what basis?

5. **Once the money is in, your leverage is almost gone.**

This is perhaps the most important structural lesson in this chapter.

The moment funds are released and pre-production begins, the ability to course-correct shrinks dramatically. Crew is hired, schedules are locked, and the momentum of a film about to shoot makes reversal nearly impossible without catastrophic cost.

This means that all of your most important questions — about budget oversight, casting authority, distribution rights, and team accountability — must be answered before you sign anything. Not after. Not during. Before.

6. Do not confuse silence for power.

Some of the most dangerous people in any room are the ones who say very little but project an air of authority.

Vagueness is not sophistication. Cryptic answers are not wisdom. Studio name-drops are not guarantees.

When someone speaks in half-sentences and lets silence fill the room, ask yourself: are they being thoughtful, or are they being evasive? Ask direct questions and insist on direct answers. If you cannot get them, do not write the check.

7. Appearances of perceived power are not the same as quiet, earned authority.

The people who have genuinely built something tend to be straightforward, specific, and comfortable being questioned. The people who perform power tend to be impressionistic, evasive, and resistant to scrutiny. Learn to tell the difference. Your instincts already know it. Trust them. Common sense is your greatest due diligence tool — and it costs nothing.

Chapter 5 –
They Sold Our Film — And Forgot to Tell Us

Distribution Opacity and the Danger of Doing Business with Friends

This story is about the distribution journey of the medical thriller in Chapter 4. In 2004 we had already lost once on that production, when we discovered that investor funds had been quietly used to finance two other films. This is the second loss. Same film. Different wound.

By the time we finished the film and turned our attention to selling it, my mother and I had been international sales agents for the better part of two decades. We knew the distributors. We knew the buyers.

We knew the territories, the price points, the deal structures, the personalities on the other side of every negotiating table in every major market in the world. If there was one arena where we felt completely safe, it was this one.

That confidence, it turned out, was its own kind of vulnerability.

The other producers on the film — the ones who had grown close to the investor during production — had significant influence over where the film would be placed for distribution. After some deliberation, we all agreed on a sales company with genuine credentials: they had sold films to Lionsgate, to major studios, and they projected confidence that our film would generate at least five times its original budget. It felt feasible. I intended to be proactive, leveraging my own buyer relationships to funnel offers to the sales agent for them to close. I knew these people. I had worked alongside them for years. I felt, if not entirely in control, at least secure.

The first red flag appeared quietly. I brought in an offer from an Italian distributor I had a longstanding relationship with — a serious buyer, a real offer, a fair price for the territory.

The sales agent did not conclude the deal. Instead, they went with a different Italian distributor at a lower price. No explanation. No consultation.

I suspected immediately what had happened, because I knew how this business works in ways that most investors never learn. Sales agents frequently sell films in packages

— bundling multiple titles together and selling them as a group to a distributor. In those arrangements, the price allocated to each individual film rarely reflects its actual market value. A smaller, more commercially viable film might be undervalued so that a bigger-budget title in the same package can command a higher allocation. Your film becomes a bargaining chip in someone else's deal.

The package serves the sales agent's overall portfolio relationship with the buyer. Your return is a secondary consideration at best.

I protested. I asked the investor and the other producers to question what was happening. They remained confident. The sales agent was their choice, and the friendship and proximity that had developed during production meant my concerns were received as anxiety rather than expertise.

Then a US sale that had been described as nearly certain simply vanished. No explanation. No follow-up. Gone.

The film made perhaps a fifth of what had been projected. And then came the news that confirmed everything.

A writer I knew in Switzerland — a client, a friend — called me, excited. He had found a DVD of our film in a store. He had bought it. He had watched it. He was calling to tell me how much he loved it. I asked him where, exactly, he had found it. He named a chain of stores — the Swiss equivalent of a video rental shop — in German-speaking Switzerland. I told him that was not possible.

We had not sold the film to Switzerland. We had not sold it to the German-speaking territories at all.

He held the DVD in his hands as we spoke. Our film. Our title. Our names. In a country where we had never authorized a sale.

When I confronted the sales agent, the explanation arrived with the practiced smoothness of something that had been prepared in advance.

They had done a deal with a German-Swiss distributor — no advance, profit-sharing only. They had been confident the film would earn money.

They had not felt it necessary to inform us or seek approval. Profit-sharing with no advance is, in the film industry, almost always a guarantee of seeing nothing.

The distributor has no financial commitment, no urgency, no accountability.

The film sits in their catalogue, technically available,

generating trickles of revenue that never reach a threshold that triggers a payment to anyone further up the chain. We never saw a single dollar from Germany or Switzerland. Nor from several other territories where, we gradually pieced together, similar arrangements had been made without our knowledge.

When we began sending letters — documenting what had happened, naming what we believed were clear violations of our agreement — the response was not an explanation or an apology. It was a legal notice. Their attorney informed us that we had no standing to make such claims, because the other producers and the financier had been aware of the deals and had raised no objection. The strategy was transparent: if the people with the financial relationship had signed off, our expertise and our contractual interests were irrelevant. The best defense, apparently, was to attack.

We were bullied into silence by people who knew we were right and calculated that we lacked the leverage to prove it at a cost worth bearing.

The sales company still contacts us periodically when they hear we are attached to a new project. I respond each time with the same message: I am still waiting to see money from that earlier film. The response is always the same. Silence. Until the next project appears on their radar. They have a short memory. Or perhaps they simply do not care. In this business, a film is an asset on a balance sheet. Your film, sitting in their catalogue unsold or undersold, may be helping them secure a bank loan against their total holdings. Their employees are being paid. Their lights are on. And your return, and your dignity, are not their problem.

What This Story Teaches Every Investor

1. **Demand a full list of every distributor and every deal — in writing, in real time.**

As an investor, you have the right to know exactly where your film has been sold, to whom, for how much, and on what terms. Build into your investment agreement a requirement that the sales agent provide a complete, updated deal memo for every territory sale within thirty days of signing.

Include the name of the distributor, the territory, the advance paid, the release window, and the platform or format of distribution. If a sale is made without your knowledge and without notification, that is a breach. Treat it as one.

2. Know the release window — and hold the sales agent to it.

Every distribution deal includes a release window: the period during which the distributor has the right to release the film in their territory. A deal with a long window and no minimum release obligation allows a distributor to sit on your film indefinitely while blocking any other sale in that territory. Require that all distribution agreements include a minimum release date, a defined window with reversion rights if the film is not released within that period, and your right to approve or at minimum be notified of any deal before it is signed.

3. Profit-sharing with no advance almost always means no money.

When a sales agent places your film with a distributor on a profit-sharing basis with no upfront payment, the distributor has made no financial commitment. They have no urgency to market it and no accountability if it underperforms.

Profit-sharing arrangements should never be entered into

without your explicit knowledge and approval.

Any deal structured this way should trigger immediate scrutiny.

4. Package deals can bury your film's value inside someone else's negotiation.

Sales agents routinely bundle multiple films together and sell them as packages. In these arrangements, the price allocated to your film is determined by the agent, not the market.

A commercially strong film may be deliberately undervalued to make a weaker title in the same package look more attractive. Ask your sales agent directly whether your film will ever be included in a package sale, and if so, require pre-approval and a minimum floor price for your title before any package can be finalized.

5. Expertise in the room is not the same as authority in the room.

In this story, the people with the deepest knowledge of distribution were sidelined by the people with the closest relationship to the investor.

Proximity to money frequently overrides professional expertise when decisions are being made. As an investor, ensure that the most qualified voices in your production are empowered to act —not just consulted and then ignored. If the distribution experts on your team are raising concerns about a deal, listen. That is precisely what you engaged them for.

6. Do not do business based on friendship. Do business based on track record.

According to Robert Greene in "The 48 Laws of Power" collaborating with adversaries can sometimes be more prudent than teaming up with friends, since friends tend to believe their connection grants them liberties that would not be acceptable in a strictly professional setting. In the film industry this plays out constantly. A sales agent who is friendly with your co-producer, or who shares a cultural bond with your investor, will lean on that warmth as a substitute for accountability. Choose your distribution partners based on verified track record, deal transparency, and contractual obligations — not on how comfortable the room feels when you meet them.

7. **When something feels wrong, document everything immediately.**

The moment you suspect a deal has been made without your knowledge, that a sale has been undersold, or that your film is being placed in ways that do not serve your interests, begin building a paper trail.

Save every email. Document every conversation in writing with a follow-up confirmation. Send formal letters through your attorney. Do not wait and hope the situation resolves itself. In this business, the person who has the documentation wins — and the person who waited to act often finds that the window for recourse has quietly closed.

Chapter 6 –
When Music Rights Kill a Movie

The Hidden IP Gatekeepers

Not every story in this book ends with a villain. Some of the most instructive ones end with something harder to process everyone did the right thing, the relationships survived intact, and the film still did not get made. This is one of those stories. I share it not as a warning about bad actors but as a warning about a trap that has nothing to do with bad intentions — and that catches investors completely by surprise.

The trap is music.

Let me start with a pattern I have seen repeat itself throughout my career, especially with newer writers. When a screenwriter sits down to craft a scene — a montage, an emotional turning point, a road trip, a first kiss — they often reach instinctively for a beloved song. A famous one. An A-list artist.

Something that perfectly captures the feeling they are trying to create.

They write it into the script as if the music were simply part of the story, as if licensing it for a film were a minor administrative detail, perhaps a few hundred dollars and a phone call.

It is not. It is one of the most complex, expensive, and unpredictable processes in the entire film industry.
To use a popular song in a film, you must clear rights with multiple separate parties: the recording artist, the record label that owns the master recording, the songwriter, and the publishing company that controls the composition rights. Each of these parties negotiates independently.

Each can name a price that bears no relationship to your film's budget. And the cost for global rights — meaning the right to show your film in every territory around the world— can easily equal or exceed the entire production budget of a modestly financed independent film. I have seen it happen. It is not an edge case. It is a recurring reality that newbie writers almost never anticipate and that investors almost never think to ask about.

Now let me tell you about the project that brought this lesson closest to home for us.

In 2012 a literary manager we respected submitted a script built around a beloved 1980s band. The story was wonderful — a coming-of-age tale about a mother and daughter, funny and heartfelt, set against the soundtrack of that era in the spirit of films like Sixteen Candles or The Breakfast Club. The band's music was not incidental to the story. It was the story. Like the city in Sex and the City, the band and its music were a protagonist. The emotional architecture of the film depended on those specific songs, in those specific moments, evoking that specific era.
We loved it immediately. Then we realized it could work when we connected with the band.

Through a manager we knew, we were able to get the script in front of the band themselves. They read it. They loved it. For them it represented something beyond a film credit — it was a chance to introduce their music to a new generation, the kind of cultural moment that artists like Prince, Madonna, and Michael Jackson have inspired long after their commercial peaks. The band was enthusiastic.

They wanted to be executive producers. They were ready to give their blessing. We met with them. We met with the manager of the band who had seen the opportunity from day one, and the manager of the director we had secured.

The energy in those rooms was electric.

Everyone was aligned. Everyone believed in the project.

All that remained was what we thought of as the administrative task of securing the music rights.

It was not an administrative task.

The band's catalogue was split between two different record labels. One label controlled their earlier recordings — the iconic songs from the 1980s that formed the emotional spine of the film.

Another label controlled their more recent work from the 2000s onward. We began making calls to understand what licensing would realistically cost.

The label controlling the 1980s catalogue — the most crucial songs, the ones that set the tone for entire scenes and anchored the film's finale— declined. Not reluctantly, not after lengthy negotiation, but firmly.

And the price they quoted for even attempting the conversation was significant: not just the licensing fee itself but legal costs, administrative layers, and conditions that made the path forward prohibitively complex. The band's own enthusiasm and executive producer involvement carried no weight with the label. The label owned the masters. The band did not control them.

We engaged a highly respected music producer, someone with deep relationships in the industry and genuine confidence that rights from other celebrated 1980s artists could be obtained within a workable budget. And perhaps they could have been. But without the band's own signature songs — the ones that had made the story worth telling in the first place — the film lost something irreplaceable.

You cannot make a story about a band's music without the band's music.

There was no wrongdoing in this story. Not from the band, not from their manager, not from the label — not even from the label that said no. Everyone involved acted within their rights and within the norms of the industry. We were all disappointed. The band was disappointed. Their manager was disappointed. The script's literary manager was disappointed. We had come genuinely close to something special, and we all felt the loss of it.

We remain in warm contact with the band, their manager, and the manager of the writer to this day. The relationships survived because the integrity on all sides was real.

And I will say this: the film may yet be made. The story is still there. The band is still there.

Sometimes the right project simply needs the right moment. We have not closed that door. We have simply left it open for now.

But as a cautionary tale for investors, this story is unambiguous. A film that could have been the next great coming-of-age comedy — something in the tradition of the films that defined a generation — was stalled not by fraud, not by incompetence, not by a bad actor in a conference room, but by the invisible architecture of music rights that nobody had fully mapped before the project began attracting serious attention and serious money.

That is the trap. And it is more common than anyone outside this industry would ever guess.

What This Story Teaches Every Investor

1. **Music rights are not an afterthought — they are a budget item that can kill a film.**

Before you invest in any film that features popular music — whether as a central element of the story or simply as background in a scene — you must understand the full cost and complexity of securing those rights. This means asking specifically: which songs are in the script, who owns the master recordings, who owns the publishing rights, what is the estimated cost for worldwide licensing, and has any preliminary conversation with the rights holders already taken place? If those questions cannot be answered clearly, the music budget is not real yet — and neither is the film's financial plan.

2. **The artist's blessing is not the same as the label's permission**.

This is one of the most misunderstood realities in the music licensing world. An artist can love your project, agree to be an executive producer, and enthusiastically endorse the use of their songs — and still be completely unable to grant you the rights. In most cases, the master recording rights belong to the record label, not the artist.

The artist's approval is meaningful and valuable, but it does not override the label's ownership. Always trace the rights to their actual legal owner before assuming any deal is possible.

3. **A song costs money every time it is heard — even when no one is singing.**

Many investors and even some producers do not realize that music clearance applies in situations far beyond the obvious. If an actor hums a copyrighted melody, if a radio plays in the background of a scene, if a character mouths the words to a famous song without musical accompaniment — all of these require clearance. The rights attach to the composition itself, not just to the recorded performance.

When reviewing a script as a potential investor, pay attention to every mention of music, however casual it seems on the page.

4. **Music rights must be cleared territory by territory for global distribution.**

Securing the right to use a song in the United States does not automatically grant you the right to use it in the United Kingdom, Japan, Australia, or anywhere else. International music licensing is a separate and often equally complex process, with different rights holders, different rates, and different legal frameworks in each territory.

A film with uncleared international music rights cannot be

sold to international distributors — which means a significant portion of your potential return is blocked before the film even reaches the market. Ask specifically about worldwide clearance, not just domestic rights.

5. **Budget inflation is a hidden risk when music rights are unresolved.**

When a production moves forward without fully costing out its music rights, one of two things tends to happen: either the music budget balloons unexpectedly and consumes funds allocated to other parts of the production, or the uncleared songs must be replaced at the last minute with lesser alternatives that compromise the creative vision of the film.

Both outcomes affect the quality and commercial potential of your investment. Require that a music clearance estimate — prepared by a qualified music supervisor or entertainment attorney — be included in the budget before you commit any funds.

6. **Not every stalled project is a failure of integrity**.

This chapter exists partly to remind investors that the film industry is genuinely complicated — that good people working in good faith on a wonderful project can still run into walls that no amount of passion or professionalism can move. Not every deal that falls apart represents fraud or negligence. Sometimes the obstacle is structural, legal, and simply beyond anyone's control. The lesson is not to assume the worst when a project stalls, but to ask precise questions that distinguish between a solvable problem and an insurmountable one.

Music rights, in some cases, can be the latter.

Chapter 7 – The Bruce Willis That Wasn't There

Fake Star Attachments and Anatomy of a Film Fraud

This is the chapter I have been most careful about telling. The person at the center of it as a victim is someone I care about deeply, a client and a friend whose trust in me I took seriously, and whose loss I still feel.

For many years as an international sales agent, I built relationships with some of the most significant distributors in the world. One of them was a client in the Middle East — a visionary businessman and genuine lover of cinema who had been part of the financing behind films like La La Land, Twilight, and that I now was advising and representing in his acquisitions of films.

He was an early rights buyer — someone who would acquire the distribution rights for his territory at the script stage, before production began, because he believed in the material and wanted to be part of bringing it to his audience.

He hired me to help him find new projects — to use my relationships and my judgment to identify the gems before the market discovered them. I took that responsibility seriously.

And then a project came across my desk in 2019 that appeared, on every surface, to be exactly what we were looking for.

The film had Bruce Willis attached to star.

Everything That Should Have Made It Safe

Let me be honest about why we trusted this as much as we did. The producers had a track record. We had met them at the Cannes Film Festival — the most credible marketplace in the world — and they had legitimate credits behind them. The project was being handled by a sales company with a real history of placing films with major buyers.

And behind the deal was a bank that discounted distribution agreements — meaning they would advance funds to producers against the value of signed contracts from distributors like my client. We knew that bank. We knew its standards. Its involvement felt like a layer of institutional validation that made the whole arrangement feel solid.

My client acquired the rights for his territory. The deposit he paid was substantial — appropriate for a film of this profile, with an actor of this caliber. He slated the film for release on a specific date, based on the delivery timeline the producers had committed to. He was excited.

He was already imagining what it would mean to bring a Bruce Willis film to his audience.

Then the delays began: The Anatomy of a Stall.

The first excuse was that Bruce Willis had committed to another project and production would need to be pushed back. A plausible explanation — scheduling conflicts happen with busy actors. Then came another delay, with another reason attached to it. And another. Each one individually defensible. Together, they formed a pattern that I began to recognize with increasing unease.

I did what any experienced professional in my position would do. I went to the source. I called the agency representing Bruce Willis.

They had never heard of the project. His agency knew nothing about any attachment to this film.

They directed me to his production company.

His production company did not return my calls.

I asked the producers to show me the contract with the

actor. What arrived was a single page — the last page of an agreement, bearing what appeared to be a signature. No identifying header. No reference to the specific film. No terms, no dates, no studio, no project title. Just a signature on a page that could have belonged to anything.

That was the moment I knew. Not suspected. Knew.

I advised my client immediately to request the full return of his deposit. And that is when the second layer of the fraud revealed itself.

The bank — the institution whose involvement had felt like a guarantee of legitimacy — had already disbursed the funds to the producers. They had discounted my client's contract and advanced the money without waiting for the full financing to be in place or for production to begin. The funds were gone. And when we traced the producers' company to pursue legal recourse, we discovered it had been registered as a shell company — conveniently dissolved, in another state, leaving nothing to pursue and no one to hold accountable.

What came next was almost darkly comic if it had not involved real money and real harm. The producers, having been exposed, attempted to offer us a replacement.

A different film. A different story. Also, allegedly, with Bruce Willis.

To prove this new project was real and in production, they sent us footage from what they described as the first day of principal photography. I watched it carefully. In the background of the shot — far away, back turned, face completely invisible — was a figure running down an alley. That was it. A person running. In the background. Shot from a distance. With their back to the camera. They were presenting a stranger running in an alley as proof that Bruce Willis was making their movie.

We never got the money back. We never got an honest explanation. We never got anything except the producers' attorney's letters accusing us of being suspicious and creating reputational harm (!), as though our suspicion were the problem rather than the evidence that generated it.

My client lost his deposit entirely. He lost the slot he had reserved for the film in his release calendar. He lost the time and the trust he had invested in people who turned out to be operating an elaborate fiction. And I carried — and still carry — the weight of having been the bridge that connected him to them, even though every reasonable indicator had pointed toward legitimacy. Thank God he also got a lot of great films through our efforts. He had been in business long enough to know that this happens in Hollywood more than once, but still.

That is the most insidious thing about sophisticated fraud. It is designed specifically to defeat reasonable due diligence. The Cannes connection. The track record. The bank. The sales company. Every layer of apparent credibility was there precisely to make the question of verification feel unnecessary. And that is the lesson that matters most.

Reasonable due diligence is not enough. In the film industry, you must go one step further than reasonable. Always.

What This Story Teaches Every Investor

1. **Verify star attachments directly with the actor's representation — every time.**

An actor's name on a project is only meaningful if the actor's representatives can confirm it. Call the agency. Call the production company. Ask for a fully executed, project-specific contract — not a last page, not a letter of intent, not a verbal assurance from the producer. A legitimate attachment will withstand direct verification.

A fraudulent one will produce excuses, delays, and partial documents.

Do not accept anything less than confirmation from the actor's own team before any money changes hands.

2. A partial contract is not a contract.

The last page of an agreement bearing a signature proves only that someone signed something at some point.

Without the full document — identifying the parties, the project, the terms, the dates, and the scope of the commitment — it is meaningless as evidence of a genuine attachment. If a producer cannot or will not provide the complete, executed agreement with an actor, director, or other key talent, treat that refusal as confirmation that the full agreement does not exist.

3. A bank's involvement is not a guarantee of a project's legitimacy.

In this story, the bank's presence felt like institutional validation. It was not.

The bank discounted the distribution contract and disbursed funds to the producers before production had started or full financing was confirmed — a practice that should never happen but does. Never assume that the involvement of a financial institution means the project has been vetted to your standard. Banks protect their own interests, which are not identical to yours. Do your own verification independently of any third-party involvement, however credible that third party appears.

4. Shell companies are fraud's most reliable escape route.

When a production entity is structured as a shell company — with minimal assets, registered in a favorable jurisdiction, and easily dissolved — it is designed to be uncatchable.

By the time fraud is discovered and legal pursuit begins, there is frequently nothing to pursue. Before committing any funds, verify the legal standing of the production company: its registration, its officers, its operating history, and whether it holds any real assets.

An entertainment attorney can perform this check quickly and inexpensively. It is one of the most important steps in any due diligence process.

5. **Escalating delays are a pattern, not a series of coincidences.**

One production delay is normal. Two is worth noting. Three is a pattern that demands an explanation — and not the kind that arrives with another excuse attached. When a project accumulates delays without a clear, verifiable reason for each one, treat the pattern itself as a red flag independent of any individual justification. Ask for a revised production schedule in writing, signed by all key parties, with specific start dates and consequences for further delay.

If that request is resisted or ignored, stop releasing funds immediately.

6. **Meeting someone at a prestigious market does not make them legitimate.**

Cannes, Sundance, Berlin, The American Film Market — these markets are attended by thousands of people, including some who are there specifically because the credibility of the venue lends credibility to their pitch by proximity. A business card from Cannes is not a credential.

A track record of completed, delivered, commercially released films is.

Judge every producer by their specific, verifiable history —
films you can look up, distributors you can call, deals you
can confirm. The prestige of the setting where you met
them is irrelevant.

7. When something feels wrong, act immediately —
do not wait for certainty.

In this story, the window for recovery closed before we
fully understood what we were dealing with. By the time
the fraud was confirmed, the money had been disbursed,
the company had been dissolved, and the legal path had
been blocked. The instinct that something was wrong
arrived earlier — in the pattern of delays, in the
evasiveness, in the partial document. Trust that instinct the
moment it appears. Ask for your money back, or freeze
further disbursements, at the first sign of a pattern you
cannot explain. The cost of being wrong about a legitimate
delay is embarrassment. The cost of waiting too long when
the fraud is real, is everything.

Chapter 8 –
The Mirage of Sales Projections

Financial Forecasting Traps

This chapter is a little different from the ones before it. I am not going to tell you a single story from my own experience. Instead, I am going to draw on something broader: years of conversations with peers, producers, filmmakers, and investors across dozens of projects and markets, sitting in rooms where the same patterns kept appearing, the same mistakes kept being made, and the same numbers kept being misrepresented to the same hopeful, well-meaning people writing checks.

The subject is sales projections. And understanding them — truly understanding them — may be the single most protective thing an investor in film can do.

The Ask and the Take

When a filmmaker approaches a sales agency to represent their film internationally, one of the first things they request — and one of the first things they use to attract investors — is a document called the sales projections.

This is the sales agency's estimate of what the film could

earn across the various global territories: Japan, Germany, France, the UK, Latin America, and so on down the list.

Every sales projection has two columns. The first is called the Ask — the best-case scenario, the optimistic ceiling of what each territory might pay if everything goes perfectly. The Take is the agency's realistic minimum, the lowest outcome it expects to achieve. The gap between these two numbers is almost always significant.

And filmmakers, when presenting their projects to investors, have a consistent and deeply human tendency to lead with the Ask. The probability of achieving every Ask amount across every territory simultaneously is, in the current state of the film market, somewhere in the region of one percent. Not ten percent. One percent.

This is not necessarily dishonesty on the filmmaker's part. It is optimism, selection bias, and the natural human instinct to present the most exciting version of a story. But for an investor making a financial decision, the Ask column is not a projection. It is a dream. The Take column — and realistically, something between the Take and the midpoint— is where your planning should begin.

The Distribution Expenses Nobody Mentions.

Before a single dollar of revenue reaches the filmmaker or the investor, the sales agency deducts what are called distribution expenses — the costs associated with taking the film to the international film markets.

These include booth fees, travel, promotional materials, market registration, and more.

Here is what most investors do not know: these expenses are charged per film, as a flat fee, regardless of how many films the sales agency is bringing to the market. If a sales company attends Cannes with fifty films in their catalogue, each filmmaker pays their allocated market expense independently — as if they were the only film being represented.

The agency does not divide the actual cost of attendance by fifty. They charge each filmmaker a fixed amount and collect it from the first revenues of each film.

The practical consequence of this is straightforward: a sales agency with a large catalogue has effectively pre-paid its market attendance costs before a single sale is made. They have already made money from your film before it sells a single territory. This does not make every sales company predatory — but it does mean that their financial incentive to maximize your film's sales is somewhat less urgent than a filmmaker or investor might assume.

The Long Contract and the Bank Loan You Did Not Know You Were Financing.

When a sales agency signs a film to their roster, they will typically request a contract term of ten to fifteen years. This surprises most filmmakers and nearly all investors, who assume such a long commitment reflects the agency's confidence in the film's longevity and earning potential. It does not. In most cases, a film will generate most of the whatever revenue it will ever earn within its first two years of release. After that, its market value depreciates sharply.

A film that commanded significant advances in year one may be worth a fraction of that by year three, and almost nothing by year five in most territories.

So why do sales agencies want fifteen-year contracts?

Because those contracts are assets. A signed agreement with a filmmaker, regardless of the film's actual commercial performance, can be presented to a bank as a revenue-generating instrument for the duration of its term. Sales companies use their catalogues of long-term filmmaker agreements to secure operating loans — loans that pay their staff, cover their overheads, and keep their lights on. Your contract may be helping someone else's company survive, regardless of whether your film ever earns a meaningful return.

This does not mean long-term contracts are always wrong. Some films — faith-based films, family films, animation — genuinely do have long commercial shelf lives and benefit from sustained representation. But the length of a contract should be negotiated based on the realistic commercial profile of your specific film, not accepted as a standard term without question.

The Advance That Arrives Too Late.

In the earlier days of international film sales, a distributor who committed to a film would pay a deposit immediately — a meaningful upfront sum that gave the filmmaker and investor early confirmation that the deal was real and the money was moving.

That practice has largely disappeared. Today, in most cases, the advance payment is completed only when the film is fully delivered — which can be a year or more after the initial agreement was signed. In the intervening period, the market shifts. The genre that was in demand when the deal was struck may have cooled. The streaming platforms that drive so much of the international market may have changed their acquisition priorities. A film popular at sale may reach a market that has already changed.

And when that happens, distributors renegotiate. They come back to the table with lower numbers, citing changed market conditions, reduced demand, or simply the reality of what they can now achieve. What can you do? Usually, you accept the new terms or lose the deal. What you saw on the projection sheet — the number that excited the investor, that justified the budget, that made the whole enterprise feel viable — is no longer the number on the check.

Box Office and the Illusion of Transparency.

Box office revenue is perhaps the most misunderstood number in all of film investment. The gross figure — the headline number that appears in trade publications and entertainment news — is not what reaches the filmmaker or investor. By the time theatrical revenues flow through the exhibitor, the distributor, the sales agent, and the production expenses, the amount that arrives at the back end is a fraction of what the front-end number suggested.

Outside the United States, tracking this is even more difficult. International box office reporting varies widely in its transparency and accuracy. Distributors in many territories will present detailed expense reports that significantly reduce the net revenue available for distribution up the chain. Percentages that looked meaningful on paper get depreciated year by year as the film ages in their catalogue. The money that was supposed to follow your investment home often gets lost somewhere in a very long and opaque chain.

Key Insights for Investors Regarding Sales Projections The requested amount represents an upper limit rather than a guaranteed commitment. Plan from the Take downward. When a filmmaker presents you with sales projections, always ask to see both columns — the Ask and the Take — and base your investment decision on the Take, not the Ask. Better still, ask what a realistic midpoint looks like, and then ask an independent consultant to validate even that number against comparable films in the current market. The best-case scenario is useful context. It should never be the basis for a financial commitment. Ask for a full breakdown of distribution expenses before signing anything.

Before your film generates a single dollar of revenue for you, the sales agency will deduct its distribution expenses. Ask for a complete itemization of what those expenses are, how they are calculated, and whether they are charged as a flat fee or as a genuine proportion of actual costs. Understand exactly how much comes off the top before you see anything, and factor that figure into your return expectations from the beginning.

Negotiate the contract length based on your film's realistic shelf life.

Do not accept a fifteen-year distribution contract as a standard term without scrutiny. Ask the sales agency to justify the length based on the commercial profile of your specific film. A five to seven year term with options for renewal based on performance is generally better suited for most narrative features and offers greater protection for your interests. If the agency insists on a longer term, ask why — and consider whether the answer serves your film or their balance sheet.

Understand when and how you will actually be paid.

Ask specifically: when does the advance get paid? What triggers payment? What happens if the market shifts between the signing of the deal and the delivery of the film? Are there renegotiation clauses, and if so, what protections do you have? The timing of payment is not a minor administrative detail — it is a central element of your investment's financial structure. Know it precisely before you commit.

Hire an independent consultant before accepting any sales projection.

A knowledgeable consultant can provide accurate data on how similar films perform in each market, including cinema, TV, and digital platforms. Not how they were projected to perform.

How they actually performed. This distinction is everything.

The cost of a qualified consultant is trivial relative to the investment being protected. Do not skip this step.

A comparable film's performance is a reference point, not a guarantee.

You will often hear the argument: this film is like that successful film, therefore it should perform comparably.

This logic is comforting and almost always misleading.

Market conditions, timing, cast profile, genre saturation, platform availability, and dozens of other factors determine a film's performance in any given territory. Comparables are useful for establishing a general range.

They are not a reliable forecast. Treat them as one data point among many, never as a promise.

Copyright is your most durable asset — protect it accordingly.

Think of a film the way you would think of real estate. When you invest in a property alongside other partners, you do not own the deed outright — but you own a documented, legally recognized percentage of the asset. A film works the same way. Whatever happens in the distribution journey — however the projections fall short, however the market shifts, however the advances are delayed or reduced — a well-made film remains an asset. Faith films, family films, animated films, and stories built around universal themes tend to have the longest shelf lives and the most durable value over time. Your percentage of ownership in that film, clearly documented in your investment agreement, is your stake in something real. It can depreciate, it can be licensed again, it can find new audiences on new platforms.

Unlike a bad stock, it does not simply disappear. Make sure your ownership percentage is legally protected, clearly defined, and cannot be inadvertently diluted or surrendered through the terms of any distribution agreement signed on your behalf. You may not own the copyright outright — but you own your share of what it is worth. That is a meaningful thing, and it deserves to be treated as one.

Chapter 9 –
When Producers Pay Themselves First

Budget Inflation and the Question of Skin in the Game

There is a phrase in Hollywood that cuts through a great deal of noise very quickly. It is four words, and when you learn to apply it, it will protect you from one of the most common and quietly devastating traps in film investment.

"Do you have skin in the game?"

It means simply this: have you put your own money, your own time, your own resources on the line for this project? Or are you asking me to be the only one taking the risk?

The question is aimed squarely at the producer. And the answer — the honest, specific, verifiable answer — will tell you more about the health of your potential investment than almost any other single piece of information.

What a Producer Fee Should Look Like.

Producing a film is genuinely difficult work. It can take years — sometimes a decade — from the moment a producer falls in love with a story to the moment it reaches an audience. The development process, the assembly of the creative team, the navigation of rights, financing, casting, production, post-production, and distribution represents an enormous investment of time, expertise, and professional capital.

Experienced producers with strong track records, deep relationships, and demonstrated ability to deliver films on budget and on time deserve to be compensated for that.

So let us be clear: producer fees are legitimate. They are a normal and necessary part of any film budget. A seasoned producer with real credits and real results has earned the right to charge accordingly.

The problem arises when the fee does not match the experience. Or when it consumes a disproportionate share of the budget. Or when it is the only line item in the budget that the producer has any personal investment in protecting.

As a rule, total producer compensation across all producers attached to a project should not exceed ten to twelve percent of the total budget.

On a one-million-dollar film, that means no more than one hundred to one hundred and twenty thousand dollars in combined producer fees. A producer fee of three hundred thousand dollars on a one-million-dollar budget is not compensation — it is a red flag.

The Emerging Producer Trap.

Experienced producers are not the primary concern here. The concern is the emerging producer — someone earlier in their career, with fewer credits and less proven judgment, who has found a strong script or an exciting concept and is now seeking investment to make their first or second film with very little work and preparation.

There is nothing wrong with backing an emerging producer. Some of the best films ever made were produced by people doing it for the first or second time. Passion, vision, and hunger are real assets. But they do not justify a fee structure designed as if the producer were delivering their tenth film with a guaranteed distribution deal already in place.

Watch for the producer who presents you with a fully formed budget, a generous fee for themselves built into it, and no evidence that they have personally contributed anything to the development of the project.

No money spent on script development. No relationships invested to attract the director or the cast. No personal financial commitment of any kind. Just a great idea, a solid pitch, and a request for you to write the entire check.

If a producer believes in their film enough to ask you to invest in it, they should believe in it enough to have already invested something themselves. Even a small check. Even deferred work done at their own expense. Belief without sacrifice is just enthusiasm.

The Producer's Pool and the Long Game.

Beyond the upfront fee, producers participate in what is called the producer's pool — a share of the film's net revenues once the investor has been recouped and other prior claims have been satisfied. This is how a producer who genuinely believes in a film makes their real money: not just from the fee, but from the film's long-term performance.

A producer who is focused entirely on maximizing their upfront fee is a producer who is not particularly confident in the film's revenue potential.

A producer who is willing to defer a portion of their fee, reduce it in exchange for a larger back-end participation, or invest some of it back into the production is a producer who believes the film will make money. That alignment of interests is exactly what you want to see.

Also be aware that films often attract multiple producers, each with their own credit and their own fee expectation. In those situations, the fees do not multiply — they must be shared from the same pool. Producers who are unwilling to share that pool equitably are telling you something important about how they view collaboration and how they will behave when money is on the table.

What Every Investor Must Ask About Producer - Compensation.

Ask directly: what have you personally invested in this project?

Before you write a check, ask the producer to account for their own investment in the film's development. Have they paid for script development? Optioned the rights from their own funds? Traveled to meetings at their own expense? Worked without pay to attach the director or the cast? The specifics matter. A producer who has put their

---

own money into a project has a personal stake in its success that no contract can fully replicate. A producer who has invested nothing is asking you to carry all the risk while they collect the fee.

Producer fees should not exceed ten to twelve percent of the total budget. This is a benchmark worth holding to firmly. If the combined producer fees on a project represent more than ten to twelve percent of the total budget, ask for a detailed justification. What specifically are those fees compensating? How do they compare to fees on comparable productions with similar budgets and similar producer credits? If the answer is unconvincing, the fee is likely inflated — which means less of your money is reaching the screen.

Look for willingness to defer.

A producer who offers to defer a portion of their fee — meaning they will receive it only after the investor has been recouped — is demonstrating genuine confidence in the film's commercial potential and genuine respect for the investor's position. It is one of the clearest signals of alignment between producer and investor interests.

If a producer refuses any discussion of deferral and insists on full payment regardless of outcome, ask yourself why their confidence in the film does not extend to sharing the risk.

Multiple producers share fees rather than increase them. When a project carries multiple producer credits — which is common — the total producer compensation should still fall within the ten to twelve percent benchmark. It should not be calculated per producer. If each of three producers is expecting their own full fee, the combined total may consume a quarter or more of your budget before a single frame is shot. Request a detailed list of all producer credits and their respective fees for the project, then check to ensure that the overall amount is reasonable and justified. Do they have a plan, a strategy, and a track record to match their fee? A producer's fee should reflect their specific contribution to this specific film, not just the general difficulty of producing. Ask them: what is your distribution strategy? Who are your relationships with buyers and sales agents? What comparable films have you produced, at what budget, and what did they return? The answers to these questions will tell you whether the fee represents real value or inflated expectations.

Experience, relationships, and a proven track record justify a premium.

A great script and a confident pitch do not.

Chapter 10 –
The Film That Had 80% Financing

When Ego Kills Deals.

When you have been in this industry long enough and have a certain level of visibility, people begin to treat you as though you have an endless supply of investors waiting by the phone. Producers pitch you over lunch. Filmmakers pitch you at festivals. Acquaintances pitch you at dinner parties. Everyone, it seems, is one phone call away from making their film — if only you could connect them to the right person with the right check.

In 2022, I was having lunch with a colleague some time ago when he raised exactly this kind of proposition. A film he was excited about. A strong cast. A compelling story. A budget of ten million dollars. And eighty percent of the financing already in place. All they needed, he explained, was someone to come in with the remaining twenty percent.

I asked him the question I always ask in this situation. Why not make the movie with the eighty percent you already have?

The question tends to produce a pause. The truth is, most producers won't admit that the fee structure, cast deals, and production design can't be sustained with only eighty percent of the budget. Something would have to give. Someone would have to compromise. And the people involved have decided that it is easier to find another investor than to make that compromise themselves.

Your Money Is Already Working Against You

Here is something that almost never gets discussed when a producer pitches you on filling the final gap in their financing: the investors who have already committed their money are sitting in escrow, waiting.
Their funds are tied up, often earning minimal interest at best, while the production is on hold. Each week that financing remains incomplete, investors lose potential returns as their funds sit idle instead of being invested elsewhere.

When a producer asks you to fill the last ten or twenty percent of a film's budget, they are not just asking you for money. They are asking you to resolve a problem that their existing team has been unable or unwilling to solve. Before you agree to do that, it is worth understanding exactly why the gap exists — and whether the people asking you to fill it have done everything within their own power to close it first.

The Questions Nobody Is Asking.

When a project is at eighty or ninety percent of its financing and stalled, there are almost always compromises available that the team has not yet made. A producer who genuinely believes in a film will find them. A producer who is protecting their own fee above all else will not.

Can a scene be rewritten to take place in a less expensive location without damaging the story? Can a day-player role be reduced or combined without affecting the narrative? Can the producer defer a portion of their own fee, as we discussed in the previous chapter, to close the gap?

Can an actor who is genuinely passionate about the material agree to a reduced upfront payment in exchange for a stronger back-end position?

These are not unreasonable questions. They are the questions that experienced, collaborative, investor-respecting producers ask themselves before they go looking for the last check. If a producer has not demonstrably worked through these options before approaching you, that absence of effort is information.

A team that will not make small compromises to get their film made is unlikely to make the larger ones that production inevitably demands. And that is a preview of what your investment experience will look like.

I also want to address the actor question directly, because it comes up often. Producers will sometimes argue that a specific actor with a specific fee is non-negotiable — that without that name, the film cannot be sold. This is sometimes true.

But in my experience, when the script is genuinely strong and the project is genuinely compelling, there is almost always a name actor who will respond to it at the price available. Great material attracts great talent.

If no actor of any commercial value is willing to engage with the project at a feasible budget, that tells you something important about how the market views the material — regardless of how enthusiastically the producer is pitching it to you.

A Smarter Way to Enter a Nearly Funded Film.

If you are genuinely interested in a project that is missing its final piece of financing, there is a structure worth considering that protects you while still allowing the film to move forward: come in at the post-production stage. Rather than investing in the gap before production begins, offer to provide the needed funds once filming is complete and the film exists in a rough cut.

This achieves several things simultaneously. It tests the producer's ability to start and complete production with the resources they have. It gives you the opportunity to see what you are investing in before your money goes in. And it tells you a great deal about the team's competence, their relationships, and their ability to deliver — all of which are invisible during the pitch phase and very visible once a rough cut is on the screen.

A producer who welcomes this structure is a producer confident in their work. A producer who resists it — who insists the money must come in before cameras roll or not at all — is worth examining more closely.

What Every Investor Must Ask When Filling the Gap.

Ask why the gap exists before you agree to fill it. When a producer tells you they have eighty or ninety percent of their financing in place and need you for the rest, your first question should not be how much and on what terms. It should be why. Why has the existing team not been able to close this gap themselves? What compromises have they already explored and exhausted? What specifically prevents the film from being made at the budget they currently have? The answers will tell you whether you are being asked to complete something real or to rescue something that the people closest to it no longer fully believe in.

The other investors' money is already sitting idle. That is your leverage.

If significant financing is already in escrow waiting for production to begin, the producer has a strong incentive to resolve the gap quickly — because every passing month costs the existing investors in opportunity cost and erodes goodwill.

Use that dynamic. Ask what concessions the team is prepared to make to get the film moving. If the answer is none, you are being asked to solve their problem entirely on their terms. That is not a partnership. That is a rescue.

Before committing to fill a financing gap, ask the producer to present a revised budget that reflects every cost reduction they have been able to achieve through their own efforts — deferred fees, renegotiated actor deals, location changes, crew consolidations. You are not asking them to compromise the film. You are asking them to demonstrate that they have tried. If the budget has not moved at all from the original ask, the team has not tried. If it has moved, even partially, you are working with people who are invested in finding solutions rather than finding someone else to carry the weight.

Consider investing at the post-production stage instead.

If a project is missing funds for completion rather than production, offer to come in once principal photography is finished. This is a fundamentally lower-risk position: the film exists, you can evaluate what you are investing in, and the producer's ability to manage a production has already been demonstrated. Structure your investment as a post-production bridge with a clear recoupment position and defined delivery milestones. It is one of the most intelligent entry points available to a non-industry investor — and one of the least commonly offered, which is itself worth noting.

A great script attracts great talent at any budget.

When a producer tells you that a specific actor at a specific price is the only path forward, probe that claim carefully. In my experience, genuinely exceptional material — a script that is truly compelling, a story that resonates — will attract actors of real commercial value even when the budget is modest. If no actor worth having is willing to engage with the project at a feasible price, ask yourself whether the material is as exceptional as you have been told.

The market for talent is a useful independent validation of the project's quality.

Pay attention to what it is telling you.

Chapter 11 –
When Ego Runs the Set

Casting Politics and Personal Agendas.

Hollywood has a long memory for certain things and a conveniently short one for others. The casting couch — that euphemism for the exchange of professional opportunity for personal favor — is one of the industry's oldest and most persistent problems. Despite years of public reckoning, despite the conversations that have shifted the culture in meaningful ways, it has not disappeared. It has simply learned to be quieter about itself.

This chapter is not about the most extreme versions of that story. It is about something more mundane and, in some ways, more insidious: the everyday ways in which personal relationships, romantic infatuations, and ego-driven favoritism infiltrate casting decisions and quietly destroy the commercial value of a film that an investor has put real money behind.

It happens in two distinct directions. The first comes from the investor side.

When the Money Comes with Strings Attached to a Person.

It is more common than the industry likes to admit: an investor who agrees to finance a film, or significantly increases their investment, on the understanding that a specific person — a girlfriend, a niece, a friend's daughter, someone they want to impress or reward — will be given a role in the production. Sometimes this is stated directly.

Sometimes it is implied so heavily that the producer understands the condition without it ever being spoken aloud.

The producer, needing the money, agrees. The role is created or expanded. The person is cast. And from that moment forward, the production is carrying a passenger — someone whose presence on set is owed not to their talent or their commercial value but to a personal obligation that now sits at the center of a professional endeavor.

When casting is driven by personal obligation rather than merit, the film pays the price. Every time. Without exception.

The scenes built around an actor who cannot carry them drag. The energy of the production shifts around the awareness that something is not right. The other cast members — the ones who earned their roles — feel it. The director feels it. And eventually, the audience feels it, even if they cannot articulate why.

If you are an investor who has been tempted to use a film investment as a vehicle to give someone an opportunity, I ask you to reconsider. Not because the impulse is malicious — it rarely is — but because it compromises the very thing your money is supposed to create. A great film. A commercially viable product. A return on your investment.

When the Ego Is on the Production Side.

The second direction is equally damaging and considerably more common. A member of the production team — a producer, a director, sometimes even a financier with creative influence — becomes personally infatuated with an actor or actress.

That person is cast, promoted within the production, given more screen time, shot more favorably, and treated with a deference that has nothing to do with what they bring to the film and everything to do with what they represent to the person making those decisions.

I witnessed this directly in 2006 on a production I will not name. An actress I knew well — a woman with a genuine body of work and real commercial value — had come aboard the film at a significantly reduced fee as a personal favor to the project. She believed in the material. She wanted to support the team. She gave them something that should have been treated as the gift it was.

What happened instead was this: a newer actress had been cast, someone connected to a member of the production team through a personal relationship that had nothing to do with the film. And from the first day of shooting, it was clear that the camera had been given different instructions depending on who was in the scene. The established actress — the one whose name would help sell the film, whose face audiences recognized, whose social media presence represented real promotional value — was being shot in unflattering angles, given reduced coverage, and sidelined in scenes that should have belonged to her.

She came to me. She was furious, and she had every right to be. She had sacrificed her standard rate to be part of something she believed in, and she was being treated as a supporting player in her own scenes so that someone else's favorite could have more of the frame.

She told me she would not promote the film. Not on social media. Not on the red carpet. Not in any interview. She had been disrespected, and she was not going to lend her name and her platform to a production that had treated her that way. She meant it.

And there is the investment consequence, stated as plainly as I can state it. An actor who refuses to promote a film is an actor whose commercial value — the entire reason they were cast, the entire justification for their fee, the entire marketing asset their name represents — has been neutralized. Not by the marketplace. Not by changing tastes or difficult distribution. By ego. By a personal infatuation that someone in a position of creative authority was unable or unwilling to set aside for the good of the project.

You do not get to misuse someone's generosity and then expect them to show up and sell your film.

That is not how human beings work. And it is not how investments are protected.

What Every Investor Must Understand About Casting.

Casting decisions are financial decisions. Treat them that way.

Every actor attached to your film represents a commercial calculation: their name, their audience, their social media reach, their willingness to promote. When casting is driven by personal relationships, romantic infatuation, or investor favoritism rather than merit and market value, that calculation is corrupted from the start. As an investor, you have the right to ask who is being cast and on what basis. If the answer involves anyone connected to a producer, director, or financier through a personal relationship, that connection deserves scrutiny.

Do not use your investment to cast someone. Ever.

If you are considering making or increasing a film investment contingent on a specific person being given a role, I ask you to stop and think carefully about what you are actually doing. You are not helping that person.

You are placing them in a professional environment where their presence is resented, their performance will be compared unfavorably to those who earned their roles, and their failure — if it comes — will be public. You are also undermining the commercial viability of a project you are financially responsible for.

The kindest and most financially sound thing you can do is keep your investment and your personal relationships in separate rooms.

Name actors who feel disrespected will not promote your film.

In the modern film marketplace, an actor's promotional commitment is as valuable as their performance. A recognized name who actively campaigns for a film on social media, in interviews, and on the red carpet can make the difference between a film that finds its audience and one that disappears quietly.

That promotional commitment cannot be contractually compelled in any meaningful way — it comes from an actor who feels respected, valued, and genuinely invested in the project's success.

Treat the established talent on your film accordingly, from the first day of production to the last day of the press tour.

Ask about the treatment of all cast members, not just the leads.

On-set culture flows from the top down. A production where personal favoritism is openly practiced will have an atmosphere that affects every performance, every creative decision, and ultimately every frame of the finished film. As an investor, you have the right to inquire about the on-set environment, including the treatment of cast members, the exercise of creative authority, and any potential tensions within the company that may influence the final product. These are not intrusive questions. They are due diligence on the human infrastructure of your investment.

Ego on set is a budget line item that nobody accounts for. The financial cost of on-set ego — the delays, the creative compromises, the promotional withdrawals, the damaged relationships that make future collaboration impossible — never appears in any budget document. But it is real, and it is often significant. A production where personal agendas are allowed to override professional judgment is a production that will cost more, deliver less, and generate more conflict than the numbers ever predicted. When evaluating a project, pay attention to the interpersonal dynamics of the team as carefully as you pay attention to the financial structure.

Sometimes the most expensive line item is the one nobody wrote down.

Chapter 12 –
The Festival Illusion

Aging Films, Ego, and the Red Carpet.

This is a short chapter. But do not let its length fool you into thinking the lesson is small. The promise of festival success is a consistently powerful tool for filmmakers pitching projects. And it costs investors real money, real time, and real opportunity every single year.

What Festivals Actually Do — and What They Don't.

Film festivals are genuinely valuable things. They create community. They generate critical attention. They give filmmakers and their collaborators a moment of celebration and public validation that is meaningful and earned. A positive review from a respected critic at a major festival can add credibility to a film's marketing campaign and open doors with distributors who might otherwise not have paid attention.

What festivals do not do, in most cases, is generate revenue for investors.

Approximately eighty percent of films screened at Sundance — one of the most prestigious and high-profile independent film festivals in the world — never find distribution. Not eventually. Not partially. Never.

Read that again. Eighty percent. If that is the outcome at Sundance, imagine what the numbers look like for the hundreds of smaller festivals a filmmaker might be pitching you on. The Oscars, the BAFTAs, the Golden Globes — these matter enormously for a film's cultural legacy and for the careers of the people involved. They do not, by themselves, compel a distributor in Japan or Germany or Latin America to acquire your film.

Awards are a signal. They are not a sale.

When a filmmaker tells you the film is going to win Sundance, or that it will be Oscar-nominated, or that the festival circuit will unlock distribution — they may genuinely believe it. Passion and conviction are not the same as market intelligence.

And the festival circuit, presented to you as a path to revenue, is more often a path to delay.

The Hidden Cost of Waiting

Here is what the festival timeline actually looks like. A finished film must typically be submitted to a major festival three to five months before the event takes place. If accepted, the festival screens the film during its run. If the film generates buzz, distribution conversations may begin — but those conversations take time, deals take time to negotiate, and release takes time to execute. By the time revenue begins to flow from a distribution deal secured through a festival, it is not uncommon for eighteen months to two years to have passed since the film was completed.

In the meantime, the film is aging. As we discussed in an earlier chapter, a film's market value depreciates with time. The genre that was hot when production wrapped may have cooled by the time the festival circuit is done. The cast members whose profiles were rising may have peaked or shifted. The streaming platforms that were acquiring independently are contracting their slates.

Every month spent on the festival circuit is a month the film is not earning — and a month closer to the point where it becomes significantly harder to sell unless it is leading on the Oscar path.

A filmmaker asking you to wait for the festival circuit is asking you to accept a delayed return in exchange for a outcome that is statistically unlikely and commercially uncertain. Make sure you understand that trade-off before you agree to it.

The Red Carpet Is Real — But You Can Have It Without the Delay.

Here is the part I want to say with some gentleness, because I understand it completely. One of the genuine pleasures of investing in a film — one of the things that makes it different from putting money into a mutual fund — is the experience of being part of something. The premiere. The red carpet. The photographs. The moment of standing in a room full of people who made something and watching an audience respond to it. That is real. That matters. And if that is part of what draws you to film investment, there is absolutely nothing wrong with it.

But you do not need Sundance for that experience. You do not need a major festival circuit or a year of waiting.

Ask your filmmaker to organize a local premiere. A screening in your city, your community, your professional circle. Invite the press, invite the cast, invite the people who supported the project. Walk the red carpet there. Take the photographs. Feel the pride of having backed something that exists and is beautiful and is being seen. It costs a fraction of what the festival circuit costs in time and opportunity, and it delivers the experience you were really looking for.

And then let the film go to market and start earning.

The Long Tail: Where a Film's Value Can Still Grow

I want to close this chapter on a genuinely optimistic note, because the picture of film value is not entirely one of depreciation and lost opportunity.

A well-made film, even one that struggles in its initial distribution window, can accumulate value over time through what the industry calls its library life. Footage can be licensed for use in documentaries, in retrospectives, in AI training datasets. Characters and stories can spin off into merchandise, into video games, into formats that did not exist when the film was made.

A faith film or a family film or an animated feature with genuine emotional resonance can find new audiences on new platforms for decades after its initial release.

This long-tail value is real. It is not a consolation prize — it is a genuine component of a film's asset profile, and it is one more reason why the copyright and ownership structure of your investment matters so much. The revenue life of a film is longer than most investors realize.

But it begins with getting the film into distribution — not with waiting for a festival that may never come.

What Every Investor Must Understand About Festivals.

Festival promises are not distribution guarantees. When a filmmaker tells you their film will screen at major festivals and win awards, ask a follow-up question: what is the distribution plan if the festival strategy does not deliver a deal? Eighty percent of films screened at even the most prestigious festivals never find distribution. A festival strategy without a parallel distribution strategy is not a plan. It is a hope. Make sure you are investing in a plan.

Every month on the festival circuit is a month the film is losing value.

Film depreciates with time. Market tastes shift, platform priorities change, and cast profiles evolve. A film may become much harder to sell just eighteen months after it was finished, even if it was highly commercial at first. If a filmmaker is proposing an extended festival run before pursuing distribution, ask them to quantify the risk: what is the realistic downside if the festivals do not deliver?

What does the film look like commercially in twelve months if no distribution deal has been struck? That conversation should happen before you agree to wait.

Ask for festivals that lead directly to distribution, not just prestige.

Not all festivals are equal from a distribution standpoint. Some — Sundance, SXSW, Toronto, Berlin, Tribeca, Cannes, Venice — are attended by buyers and acquisitions executives who are genuinely looking to acquire films. Others are attended primarily by filmmakers, critics, and enthusiasts.

Ask your filmmaker which festivals on their submission list are known to generate distribution conversations, and which are primarily for profile and recognition.

A targeted festival strategy aimed at the right buyers is a legitimate commercial tool. A shotgun approach aimed at every festival on the calendar is a delay dressed up as a strategy.

You can have the red-carpet experience without the festival delay.

If part of what draws you to film investment is the experience of attending a premiere and celebrating something you helped bring into the world, you do not need to wait for a major festival to have that.

Ask the filmmaker to organize a local premiere screening — in your city, your professional community, your social circle. Invite the press and the cast. Walk the carpet. Take the photographs. Then let the film go to market immediately. The experience you were looking for does not require a year of waiting. It requires a filmmaker who understands that your time and your money both have value.

Think beyond traditional distribution — the long tail is real.

A well-made film with genuine creative merit has a revenue life that extends far beyond its initial theatrical or streaming window. Footage licensing, library acquisitions, merchandise, gaming rights, and emerging formats like AI content licensing are all legitimate extensions of a film's earning potential. This long-tail value is part of what makes film a genuine asset — but it requires that the film first reach distribution and establish its place in the market.

Getting there quickly is always better than waiting for a festival outcome that may never arrive.

Chapter 13 -
The Shelf — When the Investor Becomes the Obstacle

A Note to Every Investor Before You Read the Checklist.

Every chapter in this book until now has been written to protect you — the investor. To give you the tools, the questions, the hard-won wisdom that keeps your money safe and your trust from being exploited. That mission has not changed.

But before we reach the checklist, I need to turn the mirror around.

Because the road runs both ways. And there is a kind of harm that investors do — quietly, sometimes without fully understanding what they are doing — that nobody in this industry talks about openly. I am going to talk about it now, because I lived it. And because the people it hurt most will never fully recover from it.

The Film That Had Everything

We met them in 2011 at a film festival here in Beverly Hills — two young Italian directors, enormously talented, hungry, and full of the kind of creative energy that reminds you why you fell in love with this industry in the first place.

They showed us a short film they had made. It was a remake of an Italian short, and it was remarkable — a thriller dealing with bullying, timely and urgent and beautifully crafted, the kind of work that announces a filmmaker rather than merely introduces one.
They asked for our help building a career in America. We said yes immediately. And then we said something more: let's turn this into an American feature film.

What followed was one of those rare experiences in this business where everything seems to align by grace. The writer who came aboard to develop the script worked for almost nothing, driven purely by belief in the material. The crew that signed on once we had financing worked below their standard rates — because they had seen the short, they believed in the directors, and they wanted to be part of something. The cast included names that audiences would recognize, actors who came on board as personal favors, drawn by the story and by the people telling it.

The investor was someone we had known for years. He was Italian. The directors were Italian. The subject matter

— bullying, identity, the quiet violence of adolescence —
spoke to him personally. He put up the money. And the
film got made.

It was extraordinary. Produced for a fraction of what it
looked like it cost — the kind of film where every dollar is
visible on screen, where the craft and the commitment of
every person involved elevates the material beyond what
the budget should have allowed. When it was finished, the
offers began arriving. Major international players.
Serious interest. Agents calling on behalf of the actors. The
European press was at the door.

This was a film that was ready to meet the world. And the
world was ready for it.

Then Came the Silence.

The delays started small. A bill here that was not paid. A
minor post-production cost that the investor declined to
cover, even though it stood between the film and its
release. We pushed. We waited. We pushed again.

Offers from distribution companies came in. They were
turned down, without explanation. A sales agent was
ready to sign — we had the contract in hand.
Months passed with no response. Social media campaigns

that had been promised evaporated. The actors' representatives were asking questions we could not answer. The press that had been circling moved on to other stories.

The money, we discovered, was held inside a shell company. There was no legal mechanism to compel the investor to act. No way to demand the film be released. No way to enforce the promises that had been made to the creative team, to the cast, to us.

We tried everything. We reached out to the investor directly. We went through the co-producer who was a mutual friend. We received excuses — grievances about minor costs that bore no relationship to the real situation, complaints so small they felt like a performance of reluctance rather than a genuine objection. There was speculation, as there always is in these situations, about what was really happening — a divorce settlement, a financial restructuring, something involving the shell company. We never received the truth. We never received anything that resembled a real explanation.

What we received was silence. And in the film business, silence is a death sentence.

The two directors went back to Italy. They went home carrying the weight of a film that had been celebrated in every room where it was shown and seen by almost no one beyond those rooms. The hype that had surrounded them — the promise of an American career, the doors that had seemed to be opening —curdled into embarrassment and frustration.

Their friendship, which had survived the making of the film, did not survive what came after. They sued one another. The partnership that had created something beautiful was destroyed by the aftermath of something that was never really their fault.

We were never fully paid. We never received the answers we deserved.

And the film — one of the best things we have ever been involved in producing, a film that could have changed lives and sparked conversations and launched careers — sits on a shelf somewhere, unseen, aging, becoming with each passing year a little more impossible to release.

A film that gets old is as good as dead. And this one had so much life in it.

What This Means for You

I have spent this entire book telling you about the ways the film industry can take advantage of investors. The fraudulent producers. The misused funds. The phantom rights. The fake stars. The inflated budgets.

All of it is real, and all of it deserves the scrutiny I have given it.

But investment in film is not a one-way relationship. When you put money into a creative work — when real human beings write, direct, act, light, edit, score, and pour themselves into something — you take on a responsibility that goes beyond the financial. You become the guardian of something that cannot be replaced. Not by another investment. Not by a tax write-off. Not by whatever other purpose the asset might serve sitting quietly inside a shell company.

Some investors finance films with the explicit intention of letting them sit. A tax strategy. A depreciating asset on a balance sheet. A piece of leverage in a negotiation that has nothing to do with cinema. And while the law may permit this, the human cost of it is real and it is significant.

Somewhere, a writer worked for almost nothing because they believed.

Somewhere, a director sacrificed years of their life and their most intimate creative vision. Somewhere, actors gave their faces and their talent on the faith that someone would show their work to the world.

When an investor lets a film die — quietly, without explanation, without even the dignity of a reason — they let all of that die with it.

The trap, in this chapter, is not the one set for the investor. It is the one the investor sets, perhaps without even fully realizing it, for everyone who trusted them.

What Every Investor Must Understand Before They Write the Check.

1. A film is not a stock certificate. It is a living thing.

When you invest in a film, you are not simply acquiring an asset. You are entering into an implicit agreement with every person who gave something of themselves to make it. The writer who worked for free. The crew member who deferred their rate. The actor who said yes as a personal favor. All of them made their sacrifices on the faith that the film would be seen.

While there is no legal requirement to honor that trust, it is considered a moral responsibility.

If you are not prepared to see a film through to its release, you should not finance it in the first place.

2. Using a film as a tax instrument without intending to release it is a form of harm.

Tax benefits associated with film investment are real and legitimate — when they accompany a genuine attempt to make and release the work.

When the tax benefit is the primary motivation and the film's release is never seriously intended, the investment becomes something else: a mechanism that extracts value from the creative process without returning anything to the people who created it or the audience that might have been moved by it. This practice exists. It is more common than the industry likes to admit. It leaves real damage in its wake.

Structure your investment to require release milestones, not just production milestones.

Most investor agreements focus on production: the script, the shoot, the delivery of a finished film.

Far fewer address what happens after delivery — the

distribution strategy, the release timeline, the minimum marketing commitment. If you are a filmmaker or producer reading this, build release obligations into your investor agreements from the beginning. If you are an investor reading this with genuine intentions, welcome those obligations. They protect the film, the creative team, and ultimately your own reputation as someone who can be trusted with other people's work.

3. **Shell companies can be used to shield inaction as well as assets.**

When the funds for a film are held inside a shell company with no transparency and no accountability mechanisms, a passive investor can effectively hold a finished film hostage without any legal consequence. If you are investing in a film, ensure that the investment agreement includes specific obligations around distribution efforts, a defined window within which the film must be actively marketed and released, and consequences for failure to act.

If you are on the creative side, be extremely cautious about allowing full financial control to sit in an entity you have no visibility into or leverage over.

4. When a film ages, everyone loses — including the investor.

A film that sits unreleased for years does not hold its value. The cultural moment it was made for passes. The actors' profiles change. The press interest evaporates. The distribution landscape shifts. What was once a timely, commercially viable piece of work becoming progressively harder to sell with each passing season.

An investor who believes they are preserving an asset by doing nothing is mistaken. They are watching it deteriorate. Release is not just the right thing to do — it is the only thing that creates any return at all.

The creative team's sacrifice deserves to be honored.

Behind every finished film is a chain of human decisions — people who said yes when they could have said no, who took less than they were worth because they believed in something. That belief is not naive. It is the engine of every great film ever made. When an investor extinguishes that engine through inaction, indifference, or the quiet violence of a film left to age on a shelf, they do not just lose a financial opportunity. They become the reason something that could have mattered never got the chance.

That is a weight worth considering before the check is written.

Yes, there are investors who get burned. This book exists to protect them.

But somewhere, someone is dreaming of a great story to be told. An artist wants to express something true. A film will impact someone's life in ways that cannot be predicted or planned. People are cutting their salaries and their sleep and their comfort to make it happen.

When that film sits on a shelf, the trap is not the one set by the industry. It is the one set by the person who held the key and never turned it.

That is as heartbreaking as any money lost or never made.

Chapter 14 – The Investor Survival Checklist

Everything You Must Know Before You Write that Check.

This checklist distills every lesson in this book into a single, practical reference. Work through it before committing to any film or television investment. If you cannot get a clear, verifiable answer to any item on this list, stop. Ask again. And if the answer still does not come, protect yourself and walk away. A great project will welcome your scrutiny. A problematic one will resist it.

THE PRODUCTION COMPANY — Chapters 1 & 7

- The production company is a legally registered entity in good standing — verified independently, not just described.

- The company has a verifiable operating history and is not a shell company created solely to obscure accountability.

- I have confirmed the company's registration details, officers, and legal standing with an entertainment attorney.

- All prior financial commitments, loans, and ownership agreements related to the project have been fully disclosed.

THE RIGHTS — Chapters 3 & 5

- The production company owns or controls the rights to the underlying material — book, script, life story, or original concept.
- I have seen and reviewed the full option or rights agreement — not a summary, not a last page. The complete document.
- The option has at least two years remaining, with clear renewal provisions in place.
- I have confirmed directly with the rights holder or their representative that the agreement is active and current.
- All music in the script has been identified. The cost of clearing those rights has been estimated by a qualified music supervisor.
- Music rights clearance has been budgeted for worldwide distribution, not just domestic release.
- For investments under million: the film's copyright has been assigned to me as collateral, documented by an entertainment attorney.

- For investments over million: a completion bond is in place, and the budget includes a contingency of at least 10–15%.

THE TEAM — Chapters 1, 2, 4 & 11

- I have met every key member of the production team — not just the person who pitched me.
- The producer's track record has been verified: specific films produced, budgets, delivery, and commercial results.
- Every title and credit claimed by every team member has been independently confirmed.
- The producer has demonstrably invested their own money or resources into this project's development.
- Combined producer fees do not exceed 10–12% of the total budget.
- At least a portion of producer fees is deferred until after investor recoupment.
- There are no personal relationships — romantic or familial — driving any casting decisions.
- Every actor attached has been cast on the basis of merit and commercial value, not personal favor.

STAR ATTACHMENTS — Chapter 7

-   I have verified every named actor attachment directly with their agency or production company.

-   I have seen the complete, fully executed actor agreement — not a last page, not a letter of intent.

-   The agreement specifically references this film, these terms, and these parties.

-   The actor's representatives have confirmed the attachment is current and active.

THE BUDGET — Chapters 2, 4 & 9

-   I have received a complete, itemized budget reviewed by an independent entertainment accountant.

-   I understand every significant line item and have received a clear explanation for any that are unclear.

-   My investment is designated for this film only. No redirection of funds to other projects is permitted without my written consent.

-   An independent accountant or escrow agent will manage disbursements tied to verified production milestones.

- I will not release the full investment in one lump sum. Funds are staged to verified milestones.
- The budget includes a contingency line of at least 10–15% for unexpected costs.
- I have approved the list of everyone authorized to write checks on behalf of the production.

THE FINANCING — Chapters 1 & 10

- If the project is partially financed, I have asked why the gap exists and what compromises the team has already made to close it.
- I understand exactly where all other investors' money is currently held and on what terms.
- The team has demonstrated good faith cost reduction efforts before asking me to fill any financing gap.
- If I am investing in post-production only, I have seen a rough cut of the film before committing funds.

SALES PROJECTIONS — Chapter 8

- I have seen both the Ask and the Take columns of the sales projections.
- I have based my return expectations on the Take, not the Ask.

- An independent consultant with current market knowledge ha validated the projections against comparable films.

- I understand the full breakdown of distribution expenses that will be deducted before I see any revenue.

- I understand when and under what conditions advances will be paid — not just that they exist.

- I understand that my ownership percentage in the film is a real asset, similar to owning a share of real estate, and is documented accordingly.

DISTRIBUTION — Chapters 6 & 12

- A distribution strategy has been defined before production begins — not treated as an afterthought.

- The sales agent's track record has been verified: specific films sold, territories, prices achieved.

- My investment agreement requires written notification of every territory sale within 30 days of signing.

- Every deal memo will include: distributor name, territory, advance amount, release window, and format.

- No profit-sharing deal with no advance can be made without my explicit written approval.
- My film cannot be included in a package sale without my pre-approval and a minimum floor price.
- All distribution agreements include a minimum release date and reversion rights if the film is not released within the agreed window.
- I have asked specifically about worldwide music clearance for all distribution territories.
- The festival strategy, if any, includes only festivals known to generate distribution conversations — not prestige alone.
- The festival strategy will not delay distribution efforts by more than an agreed, defined period.

LEGAL PROTECTIONS — All Chapters

- An entertainment attorney I engaged independently — not recommended by the producer — has reviewed all agreements.
- My investment agreement specifies that funds are for this project only, with written consent required for any deviation.

- My investment agreement includes specific obligations around release timeline and distribution efforts.

- My ownership percentage is clearly documented and cannot be diluted without my written consent.

- I have documented every significant conversation and commitment in writing.

- I know exactly where my money is held, who controls it, and what triggers each disbursement.

THE INVESTOR'S OWN OBLIGATIONS — The Shelf

- I am investing in this film with the genuine intention of seeing it released and reaching an audience.

- I am not using this investment primarily as a tax instrument with no intention of distribution.

- I have not made my investment contingent on casting a specific person connected to me personally.

- I understand that the creative team has invested time, reduced fees, and professional relationships in this project, and I respect that contribution.

- If the film is delivered to my satisfaction, I commit to actively supporting its release rather than allowing it to sit unreleased.

A final reminder from Alexia Melocchi:

A legitimate project will welcome every question on this list.

A problematic one will make you feel that asking them is the problem.

Trust that feeling. It is the most important item on this entire list.

Hollywood Is a Business, Not a Fantasy

A Love Letter to Storytelling because deep down, there is no business-like show business

We have arrived at the end. And I want to begin this final chapter the way I began the first one — with honesty.

Hollywood is full of people who arrived with enormous dreams and very little knowledge, who got burned, who got lost, who ended up in lives that kept them orbiting their real ambition without ever quite reaching it. It is also full of fraudsters and opportunists and the merely incompetent people who consume the energy and the resources of the creative ecosystem without contributing anything lasting to it. Every cautionary tale in this book is real. Every trap I have described has caught someone. Every loss I have written about was felt by a real human being who deserved better.

And yet.

This book is not an argument against Hollywood. It is not an argument against film investment. It is not even, at its heart, an argument against risk. It is an argument for going in with your eyes open — for bringing the same intelligence and rigor to a film investment that you would bring to any other significant financial decision, while never losing sight of what makes this particular kind of investment unlike any other.

Film is the only asset class where your investment might make someone cry. Where it might change the way a child sees the world. Where it might say something that needed to be said and was waiting for the right person to say it.

That is not nothing. That is everything.

The People Worth Backing

In thirty years of working in this industry, I have met every kind of person it produces. The fraudsters and the dreamers, the incompetent and the inspired, the ones who were in it for themselves and the ones who were in it for the story.

And I can tell you with complete confidence that the latter group exists. They are real. They are working. And they are worth finding.

The filmmakers, producers, writers, and actors who have the most longevity in this industry share certain qualities that have nothing to do with talent alone.

They are humble. They talk from their hearts. They protect their creative teams and they protect the people who back those teams. They build environments that are not toxic, not exploitative, not driven by ego or personal agenda. They think about the audience sitting in the dark, watching something unfold, and they take that responsibility seriously.

These are the people who understand that every word written, every image captured, every performance committed to film is going to outlast the moment of its making. It is going to be seen by someone who needed it.

It is going to reach forward in time in ways that no one in the production could have predicted or planned. It is going to matter to someone, somewhere, in ways that have nothing to do with box office or streaming numbers or festival awards.

These are the people worth your money. And when you find them, back them without hesitation.

Casting Spells.

I spoke recently with a wonderful producer on my podcast,
The Heart of Show Business, and we talked about a
concept I have been thinking about ever since: the idea of
casting spells.

Every word a filmmaker uses to bring a story to life — on
the page, in the room with collaborators, in the
conversation with an investor — is an act of creation. It is
language being used to call something into existence that
did not exist before. The right words, spoken with the right
intention, by the right person, create the conditions for
something extraordinary to happen. They attract the right
collaborators.

They inspire the right performances. They build the trust
that allows a creative team to take risks together.

That is what the best filmmakers do. They cast spells. They
use language and vision and passion to make something
real out of nothing. And when that alchemy works, the
result is a film that leaves a lasting image in the mind of
everyone who sees it — something that becomes part of
how they understand themselves and the world.

As an investor, you are part of that spell. Your resources are the material that allows the magic to happen. That is not a small thing to be part of. It is, in many ways, one of the most meaningful things a person with capital can do with it.

A Note to the Artists.

If you are a filmmaker, a producer, a writer, a director, or an actor reading this book — and I know some of you are — I want to speak to you directly for a moment.

When someone puts their money into your film, into your career, into your vision, they are doing something that deserves your deepest respect. That investment is not just capital. It is trust. It is someone saying: I believe in what you are trying to make, and I am willing to put something real on the line for it. No contract or fee can truly account for that act of faith.

Honor it. Every decision you make on set, in the edit, in the distribution strategy — make it as if the person who trusted you is watching.

Because in a very real sense, they are.

Their money is in every frame. Their faith is in every choice you make with it. The fire that keeps you going as an artist is often someone else's belief in you.

Do not take that lightly. Do not waste it. Do not mistake it for permission to serve yourself at their expense.

The artists who last — the ones whose names we still speak decades into their careers — are the ones who understood this. They treated every collaborator, every investor, every audience member as someone whose trust had been placed in their hands. And they carried that trust carefully.

The Red-Carpet Moment.

I want to leave you with an image. Not a cautionary one this time. A hopeful one.

Imagine the day — because it can happen, it does happen, and with the right preparation and the right partners it happens more often than the horror stories suggest — when you are standing on a red carpet. The film you believed in is being celebrated. The people you backed are being recognized for something they made together. The audience that was always the point of the whole endeavor is discovering something that moves them, entertains them, changes something small or large in how they see the world.

You are there. You were part of it. Not as a passive bystander who wrote a check and hoped for the best, but as someone who asked the right questions, protected their investment with intelligence and diligence, chose their partners carefully, and saw the project through from beginning to end with their eyes open and their integrity intact.

That is the experience this book is designed to help you have. Not just once. Repeatedly, as you build the knowledge and the relationships and the judgment that make you the kind of investor that the best filmmakers in the world want to work with.

There is nothing quite like the satisfaction of a team — the money, the creatives, the producers who conduct the orchestra — all coming together at exactly the right moment, in exactly the right configuration, to create something that will last.
Something that entertains. Something that moves.

Something that inspires. Something that makes whoever is sitting in that theater feel a little less alone.

Hollywood is a business. Absolutely. Unquestionably. And you should treat it as one.

But it is also something else. Something harder to quantify and impossible to replicate in any other industry. It is the place where stories become real, where images become memories, where a single frame of film can carry something true about what it means to be human across decades and continents and generations.

That is worth protecting. That is worth investing in.

Do both. Do them well. And enjoy every moment of the journey.

Alexia Melocchi

Little Studio Films

Alexandria Yacovlef & Alezia Melocchi

GLOSSARY

50 Terms Every Investor Must Know

The film industry has its own language — and producers, sales agents, and distributors have been fluent in it for decades before you walked into the room. This glossary gives you the vocabulary you need to ask the right questions, read the right documents, and understand exactly what is being promised to you and on what terms. Keep it close every time a new project crosses your desk.

A

Acquisition

The purchase of rights to a film or television project by a distributor, broadcaster, or streaming platform. When a distributor 'acquires' a film, they are buying the right to distribute it in a specific territory or format for a defined period of time.

Advance

An upfront payment made by a distributor to a producer or sales agent against future revenues. The advance must typically be recouped from the film's earnings before additional royalties are paid. Advances used to be paid as deposits during production; today they are more commonly paid only on delivery of the finished film.

Ask (Sales Projections)

The optimistic, best-case-scenario column in a sales projection document. The Ask represents the maximum a sales agent believes a territory might pay for a film if all conditions are ideal. Investors should always base their expectations on the Take, not the Ask. See also: Take.

Attachment

When a named actor, director, or other key talent has formally agreed to participate in a project. An attachment is only meaningful when confirmed by the talent's own representatives and backed by a fully executed agreement. A verbal commitment or letter of intent is not a binding attachment.

B

Back End

Revenue paid to producers, investors, or talent after a film has recouped its costs and prior financial obligations. Back-end participation is only valuable if the film actually earns enough to reach that point, which is far less common than front-end promises suggest.

Bankable

A term describing an element — usually an actor, director, or script — that a bank or financier will accept as collateral or justification for a loan or investment. A 'bankable' star is one whose attachment gives a project enough credibility to secure financing.

Budget (Production Budget)

A complete, itemized breakdown of all costs required to produce a film or television project, from development through delivery. Investors should always receive a full production budget reviewed by an independent entertainment accountant before committing funds.

C

Chain of Title

The documented legal history of ownership of a film's underlying rights, from the original source material through all subsequent agreements. A clear chain of title is essential for a film to be produced, sold, or distributed. Gaps or disputes in the chain of title can render a project legally unmakeable.

Completion Bond

An insurance instrument that guarantees a film will be completed and delivered on time and within budget. The completion bond company takes over production if the producer fails to deliver. Typically required for investments over one million dollars and by most reputable financiers.

Contingency

A budget line item — typically ten to fifteen percent of the total production budget — set aside to cover unexpected costs during production. A budget with no contingency is a budget built on optimism rather than experience.

Copyright

The legal ownership of a creative work, including a film, screenplay, or underlying source material. The copyright holder controls how the work is used, distributed, and monetized. As a film investor, your ownership percentage represents a share of the copyright's value — similar to owning a percentage of a real estate asset.

D

Day Player

An actor hired for a single day or a small number of days on a production, typically for minor roles. Day player costs are often overlooked in early budget estimates but can accumulate significantly.

Deferral (Deferred Fee)

An agreement by a producer, crew member, or talent to delay receipt of their fee until after the film has recouped its costs or reached a certain revenue milestone. Deferral is a sign that a team member genuinely believes in the project's commercial potential.

Delivery

The formal process of providing a completed film to a distributor in the agreed technical format, accompanied by all required materials including the master print, music cue sheets, publicity materials, and legal documents. Payment of advances is typically triggered by delivery.

Development

The early stage of a film project during which the script is written, key talent is attached, and financing is sought. Development costs are typically borne by the producer and are not always recouped even if the film is made.

Distribution

The process of getting a completed film in front of audiences through theatrical release, home video, streaming platforms, television broadcast, or other channels. Distribution strategy should be defined before production begins, not treated as an afterthought.

Distribution Expenses

The costs charged by a sales agent or distributor for representing and releasing a film, including attendance at film markets, promotional materials, and administrative fees. These expenses are deducted from a film's revenues before any money reaches the producer or investor.

E

EPK (Electronic Press Kit)

A promotional package containing video footage, interviews, behind-the-scenes material, and press information used to market a film to distributors, press, and audiences. Also known as a mood reel or sizzle reel when used at the pre-production stage to attract financing.

Executive Producer

A credit given to someone who has made a significant contribution to a film's financing, packaging, or overall production, without necessarily being involved in the day-to-day creative process. The title can represent genuine creative and financial contribution or can be largely honorary.

Escrow

A financial arrangement in which funds are held by a neutral third party until specific conditions are met. Investor funds held in escrow are protected from being used before agreed production milestones are reached.

F

Film Market

An industry event where films are bought and sold between producers, sales agents, and distributors. Major film markets include the Cannes Film Market, the American Film Market (AFM), the European Film Market (Berlin), and the Hong Kong Filmart.

Financing Gap

The difference between a film's total budget and the amount already committed by other investors or pre-sales. Investors should always ask why a gap exists and what compromises the team has already made to close it before agreeing to fill it.

G

Gross

The total revenue a film earns before any expenses or deductions. Box office gross is the headline number reported in trade publications — but it bears little relationship to what actually reaches the producer or investor after expenses, distribution fees, and prior claims are settled.

I

Independent Film

A film produced outside the major studio system, typically financed through a combination of pre-sales, private investment, grants, and co-production deals. Independent films represent the majority of investment opportunities available to private investors.

IP (Intellectual Property)

The creative and legal rights associated with a film, including
the screenplay, underlying source material, title, characters,
and music. Control of IP is the foundation of any film
investment and must be clearly documented before funds are
committed.

L

Letter of Intent

A non-binding document in which a party expresses interest
in participating in a project — for example, an actor
indicating willingness to star in a film. A letter of intent is not
a contract and should never be treated as confirmation of a
genuine attachment.

Library

A catalogue of completed films owned or represented by a
production company, sales agent, or distributor. Films in a
library can generate ongoing revenue through licensing, and
long-term distribution contracts are sometimes used by sales
companies to present their library as a financial asset to
banks.

M

Master Recording

The original sound recording of a song or musical piece, as
distinct from the underlying composition. Rights to the
master recording are typically owned by the record label, not
the artist — meaning an artist's endorsement of a project does
not grant the right to use their recordings.

Music Clearance

The legal process of obtaining permission to use copyrighted music in a film, requiring separate agreements with the recording artist, record label, songwriter, and publishing company. Music clearance must be obtained for every territory in which the film will be distributed.

Music Supervisor

A professional who oversees the selection, licensing, and budgeting of music for a film or television production. A qualified music supervisor should be consulted early in development to assess the realistic cost of clearing any music referenced in the script.

N

Net (Net Revenue / Net Profit)

Revenue remaining after all expenses, fees, and prior claims have been deducted. In the film industry, net profit calculations are notoriously complex and are frequently the subject of disputes between producers, distributors, and investors. Always understand what deductions will be made before your share of net revenue is calculated.

O

Option

A legal agreement giving a producer the exclusive right to develop and produce a film based on a specific piece of source material — a book, screenplay, life story, or other work — for a defined period of time in exchange for a fee. Options must be actively maintained and renewed; an expired option means the production has no legal right to proceed.

P

Package

A group of films sold together by a sales agent to a distributor as a single deal. Package sales can result in individual films being undervalued, as the price allocated to each title is determined by the agent rather than by the market. Investors should require pre-approval before their film is included in any package.

Pre-Sale

A distribution agreement signed before a film is produced, in which a distributor commits to acquiring the film for their territory upon delivery. Pre-sales can be used as collateral to secure production financing, but they are not guarantees of revenue — the film must still be delivered to the distributor's specifications.

Principal Photography

The main phase of film production during which the majority of scenes are filmed with the principal cast. The start of principal photography is typically the trigger for various financial obligations including actor payments and completion bond activation.

Producer's Pool

The share of a film's net revenues allocated to producers after investors have been recouped and other prior claims settled. A producer who believes in their film's commercial potential will be willing to defer fees and rely on the producer's pool for their primary return.

Profit Sharing

A distribution arrangement in which no advance is paid
upfront and the distributor instead shares a percentage of
revenues if and when the film earns money. Profit-sharing
deals with no advance almost always result in the producer
and investor seeing nothing, as the distributor has no
financial commitment to actively market the film.

Publishing Rights

The rights to the underlying musical composition — the
melody and lyrics — as distinct from the master recording.
Publishing rights are controlled by the publishing company,
which may be different from both the artist and the record
label. Both publishing and master recording rights must be
cleared to use a song in a film.

R

Recoupment

The process by which an investor recovers their initial
investment from a film's revenues before profits are
distributed. The order in which different parties recoup their
investments — known as the waterfall — is defined in the
investment agreement and is critical to understanding when
and whether you will see your money back.

Release Window

The period of time during which a distributor has the right to
release a film in their territory. A long release window with
no minimum release obligation allows a distributor to sit on a
film indefinitely while blocking other sales in that territory.

Reversion Rights

Rights that return to the producer or rights holder if a distributor fails to meet their contractual obligations — such as releasing the film within an agreed timeframe. Reversion rights are an essential protection in any distribution agreement.

S

Sales Agent

A company or individual that represents a film in the international marketplace, negotiating distribution deals with buyers in various territories. Sales agents charge distribution expenses and a commission on sales, which are deducted from revenues before the producer or investor receives anything.

Sales Projections

A document prepared by a sales agent estimating the potential revenue a film might generate across international territories. Projections typically include an Ask (best case) and a Take (realistic floor). Investors should always base financial decisions on the Take, validated by an independent consultant.

Shell Company

A legal entity with no significant assets or active business operations, used to hold rights or funds related to a specific project. Shell companies can be difficult or impossible to pursue legally if fraud or mismanagement occurs, as they can be easily dissolved with no assets to recover.

T

Take (Sales Projections)

The realistic, conservative column in a sales projection document representing the minimum a sales agent believes a territory is likely to pay for a film under normal market conditions. Investors should base their return expectations on the Take, not the Ask. See also: Ask.

Territory

A geographic region for which distribution rights to a film are sold separately. Common territories include the United States, the United Kingdom, Germany, France, Japan, Latin America, and Australia. Rights sold in one territory do not automatically extend to others.

W

Waterfall

The order in which revenues from a film are distributed among the various parties with a financial interest — typically the distributor, the sales agent, the completion bond company, senior lenders, investors, and finally producers. Understanding where you sit in the waterfall is essential to assessing whether your investment will generate a return.

Worldwide Rights

The rights to distribute a film in all territories globally, as opposed to rights sold territory by territory. Worldwide distribution deals are common with major studios and streaming platforms but less so in the independent film market, where rights are typically sold territory by territory.

Enjoyed this book?

If you enjoyed reading this book, I would truly appreciate it if you could take a moment to leave a review on Amazon. Your feedback not only means the world to me as an author, but it also helps other readers discover the book. Even a short review makes a big difference — thank you for your support!

WORK WITH ME

Alexia Melocchi is available for consulting, speaking engagements, and podcast appearances.

Podcast: The Heart of Show Business

Listen to The Heart of Show Business podcast on all major platforms for weekly conversations about the real business of film and television — straight from the people who live it

Available on all major podcast platforms

Previous Books (on Amazon and Barnes and Noble)

An Insider's Secret: Mastering the Hollywood Path

The Heart of Show Business: Your Road Map to Hollywood

For consulting inquiries, speaking engagements, or to connect:

Book a Power Hour with Alexia — a one-on-one consultation for investors, producers, and filmmakers who want clear, honest, experienced guidance on their specific project or situation. Whether you have a script to evaluate, a deal to assess, an investment opportunity to scrutinize, or simply need to know if the project in front of you is the real thing — a Power Hour will give you the clarity you need before you commit.

Email: theheartofshowbusiness@gmail.com
Have questions? Reach out at the same address — Alexia reads every message personally.

Instagram: @AlexiaMelocchiReal
Facebook: @AlexiaMelocchi
Little Studio Films: www.littlestudiofilms.com
Personal Website: www.alexia-melocchi.com

A Private Invitation

You've reached the end — but perhaps this is where your journey truly begins.

As a Thank You for reading *Hollywood Money Traps*, I invite you to enter for a chance to win a **private 30-minute one-on-one strategy session with me** — an insider conversation valued at **$350 USD**.

This is your opportunity to ask me anything about:
• navigating Hollywood
• pitching projects
• packaging for success
• finding financing
• international sales & distribution
• branding yourself in the industry
• avoiding costly mistakes
• building meaningful industry relationships

One winner is selected each month.

To enter, visit:
http://bit.ly/48QgEvj

Or scan this QR code:

Enter your name + email, and you'll automatically be placed in the monthly drawing.
I look forward to meeting one of you personally.

www.ingramcontent.com/pod-product-compliance
Lightning Source LLC
Chambersburg PA
CBHW071746150726
47998CB00005B/1829